FINDING JOY
ON THE MOUNTAIN CLIMB

One Step at a Time with God

Lori Arnold-Grine, PhD

BALBOA.
PRESS

A DIVISION OF HAY HOUSE

Balboa Press books may be ordered through booksellers or by contacting:

Balboa Press
A Division of Hay House
1663 Liberty Drive
Bloomington, IN 47403
www.balboapress.com
1 (877) 407-4847

Because of the dynamic nature of the Internet, any web addresses or links contained in this book may have changed since publication and may no longer be valid. The views expressed in this work are solely those of the author and do not necessarily reflect the views of the publisher, and the publisher hereby disclaims any responsibility for them.

The author of this book does not dispense medical advice or prescribe the use of any technique as a form of treatment for physical, emotional, or medical problems without the advice of a physician, either directly or indirectly. The intent of the author is only to offer information of a general nature to help you in your quest for emotional and spiritual well-being. In the event you use any of the information in this book for yourself, which is your constitutional right, the author and the publisher assume no responsibility for your actions.

Any people depicted in stock imagery provided by Thinkstock are models, and such images are being used for illustrative purposes only.
Certain stock imagery © Thinkstock.

ISBN: 978-1-4525-9793-5 (sc)
ISBN: 978-1-4525-9792-8 (e)

Library of Congress Control Number: 2014919325

Printed in the United States of America.

Balboa Press rev. date: 12/5/2014

Contents

Dedication

I dedicate this book to God, my true Strength and Author, and from whom all blessings flow.

Written for anyone who needs hope, strength and encouragement to keep on climbing.

May all who read… see God in my words and be encouraged.

**"Commit to the Lord whatever you do, and your plans
will succeed" Proverbs 16:3 (NIV).**

Acknowledgments

Thank you to those who have faithfully and lovingly climbed alongside me in this journey and encouraged me to keep lifting my hands up in praise to God through it all:

My parents in Heaven, Lewis and LaDonna Arnold, who were my first teachers and encouragers. They paved the way for my childhood faith by raising me in church and a loving, family-oriented home; and by supporting my education, teaching, writing, and piano lessons. I kept "Arnold" in my name to honor their guidance and gifts. I can't wait to meet up with you in Heaven some day!

My husband, Mark Grine, who has been my number one caretaker and supporter through a long, difficult health journey. He has walked alongside and supported me through all my educational efforts and dreams, not to mention his invaluable technological assistance and advice. We enjoy traveling adventures, and he took the scenic photos in the Smoky Mountains of Tennessee to use in this book. Thank you for your faithfulness and love to me for over thirty years!

My children – the lights of my life and my cheerleaders! Tiffany, the caretaker and eldest child, who listens, supports, and advises me in more ways than she realizes; and her husband, Chris Boehler, who brings a lot of laughter and character to our family! Kelsey, the spirit-filled encourager, who prays and speaks words of truth to encourage me that God has a purpose and a plan through it all; and her husband, Derek Ellis, who is a faithful servant of God and joyous addition to our family; Kaleb Grine, my delightful son who shares my love for characters and puppets, and with whom I've had some memorable adventures – most notably our visit to Sesame Street; I marvel at his intellect and graphic design capabilities (and am so honored that he designed my book cover)! It is for all of you that I role model always striving to do your best, reaching for your dreams, and keeping God as your guide, come what may. Thank you for your love and always being by my side and cheering me on!

My new additions to the family – grandson, Gabriel Christopher Boehler; and granddaughter, Avalyn Grace Ellis – both born in 2014. They have been a testimony of God's plan and timing, as they have given me a renewed purpose and hope in healing. You are my blessings of strength and love! Gigi loves you to the moon and back!

My "Sisters in Faith" and dear friends – Becky Nusbaum and Joni Jordan – who encouraged me to write this book per God's calling. They sat by me through many days of healing and coping, crying and praying together. You are amazing women of God!

Readers of my health blog – who have leaned on my words and fueled me to keep writing!

My cloud of witnesses who have inspired me in my faith journey – "Grandma" Jane Tuthill, Aunt Helen Gilliland, Rita and Larry Bennett, Pastor Jim Stauffer (and former pastors over the years) and many friends of the faith and music ministry. Thank you for helping me to see and know Jesus through your words, listening hearts and faith-filled lives.

Last but not least, my comfort kitty and faithful companion, Barney.

In His Arms

We can't always trace His plan for us;
Sometimes we can't see His hand.
Things happen that don't make any sense.
We ask, "Why? I don't understand!

But I bet He cries when we cry;
I know He feels our pain.
He understands when we're wrought with grief,
And He'll help us get up again.

He never said life would be easy,
But He promised to never leave us alone.
He won't give us more than we can bear,
With Him we're stronger than on our own.

So when your path is rocky,
And you can't see the rainbow's end,
Remember that God is holding you…
His strong arms will never bend.

Introduction

Every journey has a story. Telling my story is part of my journey and my healing. I share my story as a witness to God's continual presence and a testimony to encourage others to keep in step when the way is steep. My story is laden with scripture because throughout my health journey, God's word has been my best medicine. Reading and reflecting on scripture has brought be through a very difficult climb, even if it isn't over yet! I began writing this book when I realized that not only is writing therapeutic for me, but that God wanted to use my situation to encourage others and bring glory to Him. He never wastes a hurt! Plus, I had audible callings – through suggestions of friends – one in particular, whom God prompted to suggest to me to write a book. When God calls, we must respond in obedience. Plus, He would not bless me with writing ability (or this experience) unless He wanted me to use it for His glory. God uses everything that happens to us to shape us for our service to Him. It is only through knowing God that we can discover His true purpose for us and follow Him as He guides us to fulfill it. It's not really about me anyway, because I was made *by* God and *for* God. So what would give Him the most glory and honor Him the most? He wants me to be a voice, helping others to think about Him and lead them to know Him. My health situation has changed and been more like a roller-coaster than a diagonal ascent or climb up a mountain. I have seasons of feeling good/bad and many places in-between those labels. When I have hit plateaus of healing and recovery, I kept "stalling" – having lulls in my writing of this piece. I realize now that God was carrying me through this journey – the health one as well as what I was learning from it. I had to get to certain places in my thinking and understanding of how God was at work through my affliction to see how He wanted to use it. It has been amazing to look back and realize how He was moving. I remember the revelation one day that I was waiting for ultimate healing (or so I thought) and an end to this journey to finish the book and figuratively speaking…to reach the summit of the mountain. God spoke to me that it wasn't about a resolution, healing, or a destination. It is all about the journey, using it to help someone else, and seeking joy in the journey. That is when I decided that I needed to use my situation to offer encouragement to others and share my story. The journey is ongoing for the amount of time God gives me, so I'll tell the story while on the mountain. Joy is found in Jesus, independent of my circumstances, even when the climb is steep. And here is the key point of understanding that God brought to me in this purpose: <u>For it is within the battle that we find ourselves committed to what matters the most</u>. In my case, what matters most is that I use all my life experience and gifts to honor Him. Leading someone else to know and walk with Jesus is more important than my life alone and my comfort. God brought me to this mountain and will be with me on it. I had to take these steps to learn this truth, and I continue to learn as I take one step at a time with God. When there is a purpose, we find the mountain more worthwhile to climb…and with a greater dose of grace. This is my testimony, my story, and my song. *Lord, help me to use my voice and purpose to be a blessing of encouragement to others who are hurting. Thank you for this journey so that I might tell my story – which is really Your story. And may I always give You the glory and the praise in all circumstances.*

As a teacher, I felt I needed to have a learning objective to give shape to my writing and help me pull it together. This goal came from God's directive and gave impetus to completing this book: to share my testimony of my health journey, and to let it speak of my faith in God and how He has guided me on my mountain journey. The "moral" of the story and main point that I hope the reader will come away with is this: <u>God will carry you with peace and comfort over your mountain. He is the light for your path.</u>

The mountain climbing metaphor came from so many mountain references made during my journey. In reading back through my journaling in and around the last major surgery, I found that so often I had referred to the "mountain ahead" and to "keep on climbing" perseverance analogy. I think it also felt like such a steep and heavy road ahead that as I tried to look forward it just seemed like an uphill path, and thus, a mountain. My journaling – that turned into a health update blog – caused supporters to encourage me to put this into the form of a book. I guess it was the encouragement of my fellow climbers, who were essentially pushing me onward and upward and calling back. To "call back" – when climbing a mountain it is helpful to have someone call back to encourage others and summon them toward the top. In a relationship with God, He does the call back to encourage us to keep climbing. This term also implies that one should never climb alone. Life is steep. We cannot and should not try to do it alone. We need God's unfathomable strength and encouragement of those who are willing to step up and climb alongside us to reach the summit. We can use our experiences to, in turn, call back to encourage others. Great is the reward of comforting others, which comforts us for our climb and journey as well. Becoming the blessing is what blesses us in return. The way through pain is to reach out to others in theirs. God does not ever want us to waste any of our experiences but use them to help and love someone else, for He always has a plan for us in everything that happens. Nothing comes to us that hasn't passed through His hand first. It is my prayer that this book will be a call back to others on the arduous climb. *You are never alone.*

What happens to us in life isn't nearly as important as how we respond to what happens to us. It is all about what we do with the hand that we are dealt. I know that God has a purpose for our pathways, and there is victory in giving thanks in all circumstances and using them to do the

Lord's work. I take this purpose for writing as a way to apply **1 Corinthians 15:57, 68: "How we thank God for all of this! It is He who makes us victorious through Jesus Christ our Lord. Since future victory is sure, be strong and steady, always abounding in the Lord's work, for you know that nothing you do for the Lord is ever wasted as it would be if there were no resurrection." (TLB)** May this book be a platform from which to display God's grace, power and love; or a conduit – a channel for witnessing, sharing what God has done through my journey, and how He uses everything that happens to us for His purposes. God is writing the story and the ending, because He is the only One who knows how it all works out and where it leads. Yet I trust Him in His purpose. He is my Author. I am humbled and honored that He has chosen me to be a part of His work. My confidence is not in myself but in God's power that enables me to continue on my journey.

When we call upon the Lord, we fully hope that He will respond with an answer. So when God calls us to do something, we must obey. As He instructed Paul in **Acts 9:15, "Go and do what I say. For you are my chosen instrument to take my message to the nations…"(TLB).** I must obey the call to write this message. I have felt God strengthen me with hope through being obedient to His call, and with the intent of encouraging others it has done the same for me as I am used as an instrument. **"I thank Christ Jesus our Lord, who has given me strength, that He considered me trustworthy, appointing me to His service" 1 Timothy 1:12 (NIV).** *May God remain the fire in my heart and the wind in my sails!*

1

The Mountain

"I will lift up my eyes to the hills…My helps come from the Lord, who made heaven and earth" Psalm 121:1 (NKJV).

I've heard some compare life to a mountain, with its ups and downs. That's why a mountain climb is an appropriate metaphor for a life battle. Both need to be handled with care, one day at a time, and with Jesus. Of course we know that life is a mixture of valleys and hills, and it is not all (or even much) an easy coast downhill. We need both the valleys and the hills, for the hills make us appreciate the valleys even more! The hills and mountains of life are what drive us to the throne of grace and deepen our trust in our Savior to carry us. It is then that we realize how much we need Him and His strength. If we cower in the lowlands, afraid to ascend the mountain, we will miss the blessings of the climb and the glory of the summit.

This book is a guide for your mountain journey, but you have to do it with a heart open to God's presence with you. It is a reminder that whatever the struggle, you are never alone. Whatever mountain you are facing, it will not be an easy ascent. There will be times when you want to turn back, jump off, or just stop in your tracks. But at every point, God is there, climbing with you…in fact, ahead of you. He knows each step that you take even before you take it. His grace is sufficient, and His companionship is all that you need. In fact, God leads us up mountains sometimes so that we realize that it is only His hand that supports us. The higher we go, the more we are keenly aware of only His presence and that it is His light alone that guides us. The most difficult journeys bring us face to face with God as He calls us to lean on Him and know him at a deeper level. The only way to really survive is to grab onto God's hand and hold on tight!

Keep circling your mountain. With each step, you are one step closer to God. Put one foot in front of the other and refuse to stop until you reach the top! The top might not be what you think or even a resolution to your issue. But it is God's resolution, and He is leading the way when you journey with Him. God doesn't promise an easy climb in this life, but He promises to be with you and that the harder the climb, the sweeter the summit. You will not take the path of least resistance, but with God, the path of greatest glory. He alone is sufficient to be our strength and to guide us as we climb our mountains. We should lift our eyes to the One who will guide us and keep us safely in His care. **"I lift up my eyes to the mountains – where does my help come from?" Psalm 121:1 (NIV).** *Go forward. There is no other way around this mountain.*

I never intended to take up mountain climbing. I never even had the desire. I don't even know anything about it! Actually I never have climbed a mountain in the literal sense (except for short hiking paths), but figuratively I have faced mountain after mountain and have decided that it's a good thing that I don't know what lies beyond the next one. Thankfully only God knows what lies beyond the next one and how we will maneuver each. As I think back on those times, I did have a choice as I faced another mountain climb. Option 1: I could stay at the foot and keep staring up at it wondering why I was there and how I'd get over it. Option 2: I could face it, gear up, and start the climb. This option has often included a process of falling down, brushing myself off, and getting up to try again. Option 3: I even had the choice to quit and just stay at the bottom. I think I tried all three different approaches at one time or another. God waited patiently when I lingered at times, unsure which option to choose or if I even wanted to go on. He understood my despair and reluctance at the worst of times. The best lesson I've learned is this: *Never go mountain climbing alone.* In fact, make sure your main companion and instructor is God. Others will help you and support you, but even when you feel like you're climbing alone on your worst days – God is there, supporting you, if you let Him. It's not all that easy as it sounds or looks in print. I know, for at this moment I'm climbing yet another mountain and have no idea what I will see at the top (or if I'll even reach it). Another mountain? A Haitian proverb says, "Life is climbing one mountain after another." But God already has my course figured out to the number of steps

I will take, when I will take them, which path, where I'll end up, and how many mountains are involved. But God is already there, and there's no mountain too high for Him. There is no other way around it but to go forward. *Sometimes it feels like I'm circling the base of the mountain and getting nowhere. Or like I'm falling down – like two steps forward, three steps back. I've changed my focus about reaching the top. I know I'm not home yet, and maybe that is the top – the eternal summit. Maybe I'm on the last mountain. Maybe there are several more. But I will keep praising my Lord and Savior.* **"I will praise the Lord no matter what happens. I will constantly speak of His glories and grace. I will boast of all His kindness to me. Let all who are discouraged take heart. Let us praise the Lord together and exalt His name" Psalm 34:1-3 (TLB).**

I begin writing this book in the midst of a season of intense pain and suffering. I had always had the glimmer of a thought to write a book, but as it seemed to be coming to more of a reality, two friends (who didn't even know each other) told me separately that they felt compelled to tell me to write. I received these two messages within the same hour! I love it when God speaks so clearly! Yet, they had different topics in mind, and frankly I had been pondering those topics and grappling with the desire to write. As other authors who have written during affliction have noted, it is difficult to focus and think clearly when your mind is so hooked on the unrelenting pain. But I think the urgency and the feeling of helplessness has compelled me. My daughters encouraged me to write while the feelings are so real…or "raw" as I would put it. I don't think I could write a book like this in a different season of life, and that gives more purpose and usefulness to the pain. I am in a place that I have never been before in my pain, yet clinging to total reliance on God when no one else understands or I cannot even find the words to describe it. And what's the use? I am at a point when it seems nothing else can be done, so I must serve my Savior while I'm waiting. I'm not even sure what I am waiting on anymore. Healing? I believe in it…if it be God's will. I do believe that God will make a way when there seems to be no way. Meanwhile, I will keep seeking a close connection with Him and will write in hopes of encouraging someone else who is also dealing with a heavy burden of pain (physical, emotional, etc.) or just needs some encouragement to keep going. It is also an act of obedience to a call to service. So many times I have asked why God has emptied my hands of so much…my health, and as a result – my teaching, what seemed to be my greatest purpose. But God had another purpose in mind for me and wants to use me in this way. Who am I to question why, but to obey? I am humbled for His call to service and hope that I can fulfill the task – only with His help and guidance. It feels like an insurmountable task, but I know that His power is great when ours feels small. Above all else, I want God to get the glory!

I guess I might be on what a mountain climber would refer to as a *switchback* – a mountain road that rises and falls sharply (dictionary.com). When hikers switchback up a mountain, they proceed in sharp turns in alternating directions on the incline, trying to find their way as they climb. I'm going back and forth between doctors and suggestions, trying some things and waiting, still looking for the exit sign yet wondering if there is a way up or off this steep mountain. Eventually I tire of pacing back forth with the ole "two steps forward, ten steps back" feeling and try climbing higher. The bad pain days weigh me down like a heavy backpack, making the climb seem steeper and more difficult with a heavy load. I'd rather just curl up on the path and stay there. But apparently God's not done with me yet, and so the journey climb continues.

~

My mountain: I was going to write that it all started…then when trying to figure out approximately when this battle began I realized I really don't know. Since God predetermines our life and has every day accounted for, I guess it started way back before I was even born. But the arduous part of the physical battle with pain and discomfort probably started in my early twenties. I was thankful to have a reprieve and give birth to three healthy children. Those are some of the blessings in my life for which I am so grateful. God was building my climbing team even back then with the blessings of my supportive family – including my husband who has always been by my side and tried helping me by seeing doctor after doctor; and then eventually my children who have been understanding emotional and spiritual supporters. I was also able to teach elementary school for many years and fulfill my desire since a first grader myself to be a teacher! Later I felt a calling to earn further degrees and teach at the college level. I used my own teaching experience to train teachers. It was very fulfilling and an arduous journey in itself to get there, especially while battling a disease. The symptoms were escalating during my most intense years of juggling motherhood, teaching, and my doctorate studies.

The symptoms of the painful condition with which I have battled for many years started occurring over time, gathering momentum and intensity over years. There were stomach issues involving the bowels and the bladder. This all kind of got really going after three difficult pregnancies and a necessitated hysterectomy following the last one. Then things just seemed to get out of hand over time, and there was never an answer to why I had so much pain.

Eventually I was diagnosed with IC (interstitial cystitis) by a urologist after many bladder infections (and even negative test results) and many consultations with doctors that ended with the words, "I don't know how I can help you. The tests do not show anything wrong." One doctor even went so far as to tell me it was all in my head. Not only at that point are you so miserable from the illness but now you question if there is something wrong with your mental state! Finding a urologist who knew about IC over ten years ago was something short of a miracle. I have always thought of him as a God-send and an answer to prayer. There is no definite test for it, and the diagnosis comes after a process of elimination and discernment. A procedure called a cystoscopy (done with a scope that is inserted and then pictures can be taken inside the bladder) confirmed the irritated lining that is characteristic of classic IC. My urologist referred to mine as "textbook

IC" – meaning the pictures of my bladder could be model textbook diagrams of the condition. Then began the course of trying many types of treatments and a long process of waiting to see what worked. I tried everything available at that time – bladder instillations of medicine and anesthetic, pain management, pain patches and medicine, acupuncture, a neurological implant, etc. I would find that something would work for a while (maybe even up to six months) and then lose its effectiveness. This went on for several years, life like a roller-coaster of pain and hope, up and down all the time. (There's that mountainous image!) I even sought out other doctors and researchers in the field for their opinion. We traveled to the best medical facilities in search of answers. The pain was wearing on me and got to the point of interfering with my work, my family, and my life in general. Quality of life was low; despair was high. One gets to the point of not wanting to go on if every night and day is miserable, always putting on an act that you can handle the situation while limping along and secretly feeling hopeless. Not to mention the unrelenting pain that afflicts the body and the feelings of urgency for a normal bodily function.

Quality of life became the major issue and that needed to improve if I was going to be able to go on living with this disease. After much consultation and research, a decision was finally made (and not lightly) to take a drastic measure. In 2007 I had an ileal conduit surgery to bypass usage of my bladder. Now I urinate through a stoma and wear a two-piece external "bag-like" appliance. I change it twice a week and just empty the pouch every couple of hours via a spout as the bag fills. I urinate automatically, no longer having any control over that – but also no feelings of urgency and the pain and frequency that accompanied that painful function. Oh, there are days that I hate it, but most of the time I realize that the stoma/conduit is my lifeline. This is not something that I recommend doing for IC, but I had lost so much weight and quality of life had slipped very low. Also, the recuperation from this surgery was very hard on me, and due to other complications with resuming normal diet and body functioning, as well as some bad infections, I almost died within a few months of the surgery. It took a good year before I was "healed" to the point of accepting "the new normal" and adjusting to a new way of living. You see, I was not healed of IC, necessarily. Yes, my condition and state of pain improved greatly, but healing came in another form. I have always been a believer in God, but this experience took me to a deeper relationship with Him. In my weakness and "altered state" I needed to know that I still had a purpose for living and a reason that God kept me alive. I am a survivor for the very reason that God gives me the needed strength and calls me to reach out to others and offer hope. I knew that God would lift me to a new state of normalcy as I had to accept my new body. There is a continuum of this ongoing process of acceptance and adjustment that includes a bridge to cross over. **"So now I am glad to boast about my weaknesses, so that the power of Christ can work through me. That's why I take pleasure in my weaknesses and in the insults, hardships, persecutions, and troubles that I suffer…for when I am weak, then I am strong" (2 Corinthians 12: 9b-10 – NLT).** As Paul's words relate, I find the silver lining of this affliction has been my deeper reliance on God. As my adjustment and healing process continues, He is giving purpose to my pain and using my experience to reach out to others. I want to serve Him and give Him the glory. For though I am weak in body, my spirit in God – Who lives in me – is strong and my true Lifeline.

My body is definitely scarred. It has been drastically altered. But I continue to heal and have to face it daily. I am not sure one is ever done healing in a situation like this. People often tell me that I "look good" and ask, "Are you better?" My reply has often been that I am "adjusting to the new normal." Or even abandon the word "normal" altogether and accept it as a state of being that I am attempting to "maintain." I have had to accept my body in the present and refuse to allow my earthly condition to keep me from living life with purpose. The scars are not only physical, they are internal as well. Daily I have to chase away the feelings of "this is not fair" or the "Why me?" questions. Those thoughts rear their ugly heads often, and I have to give it to God and take up my cross daily and remind myself of His love. **"The steadfast love of the Lord never ceases; His mercies never come to an end; they are new every morning" Lamentations 3:22-23 (ESV).** I have crossed a bridge to find what a "new normal" is and give glory to God for my existence. He has a purpose for me, and He is obviously not finished with me yet on this earth. He has a purpose for each one of us, and we have to hang onto that hope and strength.

It is also very important to have a family of supporters – whether it is your actual relatives or friends or support group – people who know your story and your battles, a circle whom you can call on to intercede with and for you. It's even good to laugh with others about your situation (which might sound absurd), but it is a coping mechanism. You might not be in a place to laugh about it right now, depending on where you are on that healing bridge. My husband and kids laugh with me when we are traveling or stopping for a restroom break and I say, "I can hold it!" (You might have to think about that!) Healing of the spirit can be just as helpful as the physical kind. Why not laugh? It's good for the soul! I have also done things with my ostomy that I never thought would be possible – lots of traveling, cruises, snorkeling in the ocean, and even para-sailing! In fact, I started writing this while sitting on the beach! I am also very active in my church and up until recently when the disease took a huge toll on me, I was a professor of education at a university. I keep very busy with my family and love to take care of others.

God loves me so much and waited more patiently than I did for healing. I believe now that healing is a relative term. I'll never be pain-free completely or without complications and difficult side effects in this state. In fact, as I started writing this three years following the first major surgery and turning point, I was battling major infections. It is a challenge to the very hope that I speak of, as I remind myself of these very words: *There is hope.* But I have unspeakable joy and gratitude for life (even though some days are cloudier than others). I have been given a second chance and a renewed spirit and purpose. I'm also not afraid to die, having been at the brink of death and prepared to go Home. The joy I feel includes the confidence of where I'm going and that nothing on earth can keep me from that eternal life as long as my hope and faith is in Jesus. I choose life over pain, and thanks be to God!

I have chosen hope rather than despair. In fact, I try to look at this situation from the perspective that I have a task set before me. Faith helps me to look at my circumstances *through* God, with eyes of faith…especially when my earthly self wants to question why things are happening. There is always purpose in the pain, and God never wastes a hurt. I am a survivor for a reason. I have been chosen as an instrument of healing and to share my story with others and to offer hope. It is not only in our years of strength and youthfulness that God will use us, but as well in our sickness and weakness. We honor God by using our skills **"each according to his own ability" Matthew 25:15 (NIV).**

My situation does not define me, but it did transform me. I felt a turning point one day when I heard words to a song that said "a hero lies in me." This is true of surviving, but my hero-ship cannot be kept to myself. I can't hold onto this experience as if it were only mine. My healing path has brought me to a place where I know that I have to share this with others, and I invite you to climb this mountain. An experience like this changes one's outlook on life and life eternal. I have always been a believer, but now I feel called to minister to others who need to hear a message of hope for their health situations. **"Praise be to the Father of compassion and the God of all comfort, who comforts us in all our troubles, so that we can comfort those in any trouble with the comfort we ourselves have received from God" (2 Corinthians 1:3-4 NIV).**

My message of hope is to not let your situation defeat you. There is a bridge to cross in order to climb your mountain. Regardless of where you are in this continuum, it is important that you cross this bridge. Maybe you just need to start with taking a step toward it. Or maybe you are stuck in the middle and can't seem to cross or even take another step. Wherever you are, take a step farther and keep your eye on the light of hope; at the very least, reach out your hand to let Jesus help you. In fact, *He is the Bridge.* My goal is eternal life with Jesus in Heaven and meanwhile on earth to help others to know Him. My healing came in the Cross and the hope that Jesus offers. While I kept waiting for bodily healing, I realized while on that bridge that my healing is in God and that in life eternal my body will be whole again. Jesus will be the only one in Heaven with scars. I love that! Those same mighty hands that hold me when I'm broken will hold me in life eternal. God will not leave you or forsake you in your current state. He will never abandon you on the mountain. No burden is too big for Him to handle. That is the rope that you need to hang onto when you feel like you're sinking in your situation, regardless of the circumstances, and what hope is all about. I know that all health battles do not have the same earthly ending, and sometimes there is no hope or answer that a doctor can offer. But that is the earthly situation, not the eternal one. That is seeing life with an earthly eye instead of a spiritual one. The hero is not necessarily the one who survives here on earth, but knows where s/he is headed. The ending/

hope that truly matters is the eternal one, and that is something only God can promise. *There is hope in His healing.*

~

Interestingly, I had written the above description of my situation just before those infections got a whole lot worse and landed me in the hospital for a couple of lengthy and uncertain stays. Here started the next ascent of the roller-coaster, or the next mountain. (This was about 3 years following my original ileal conduit surgery.) I had several infections at a time, and the dilemma was to find out what was causing them or they would eventually take my life. Local doctors were stumped, and I was accustomed to being my own advocate and researcher. So the quest began, and my youngest daughter traveled with me to Mayo Clinic in Jacksonville, Florida. (We figured we'd head for the warmest Mayo climate since it was January and we are from Ohio!) A week of tests brought no clear cause of the infections, but it did open up a possibility. We met with a urologist on the first day who, after viewing my films and reports, walked in, greeted us, and said, "I think I know what your problem is!" Well, that is not something I was used to hearing, so we were instantly curious. It was good news that someone finally had an idea, but the bad news was that I now had a big decision to make and another risk to face either way. The urologist at Mayo thought my conduit that drains my urine through the stoma and into a urostomy bag was too long. He suggested that shortening it might help with drainage and keep infections from forming where urine was "pooling." Well, long story shortened (pun intended – think about that), I drug my feet and rebelled. I sought several doctors' and people's advice, but I knew what had happened in the aftermath of the first surgery. I had an awful recovery, lost weight, diet, bowel control, etc. I thought I would rather die than go through that again! My family supported me and understood, but they wanted me around and encouraged me to do the surgery. They promised to see me through, although little did we know what would lie beyond that next mountain! I wrestled with God for weeks before I surrendered, and honestly I did it mostly for my family. But I kept hearing God speak to me that He had plans for me. Once again I faced a huge risk and another bridge of faith to cross without knowing what lies beyond. But faith in God includes taking His hands for those steps and trusting you will make it. God gives us just enough light for the steps we are on and calls us to lean on Him to carry us.

Reluctantly we made the plans to relocate to Florida for a month for the surgery and recovery. I was already on medical leave of absence from the university where I was a professor of teaching, but my husband had to also take a leave from his college teaching. Our children came down for the week of surgery, and as they promised, they were a great support team. I feel like I wrestled with God right up to that point in some ways, and I told my family if I saw Jesus I was going to RUN to him! They agreed but admitted how relieved they were when I made it through the 4-1/2 hour surgery. It was grueling. The surgeon ended up taking about 22 cm (8.5 inches) off of my ileal conduit, with the plan for it to be able to drain more easily. However, there were many, many adhesions from the former surgery and when those were cut out it made a hole in my intestines that also needed a repair, including a bowel resection. (Adhesions are fibrous web-like bans that form between tissues and organs as a result of surgery. They are basically scar tissue of internal organs and can cause pain since they connect things that aren't meant to be connected.) I recall one doctor on the team apologizing to me the next day, "I am sorry. No one should ever have to be cut that much!" It sure felt that way! I was in the hospital for 11 days and on an "ice chip diet" for the first four days. It seems my bowels and digestive system could not "wake up" and even after I finally got to leave the hospital and stay nearby, I had trouble. I would have pain when I ate anything (even soft foods and liquids) and some bowel blockages that would send me into rages of pain, nausea and vomiting. We were near the ocean, so getting to the sand was my "prize" when we would take slow, painful walks to try to get things "moving." Things seemed to improve at a snail's pace, and finally after several weeks we came back home to Ohio. It was scary to be so far from help, even though I could call. The mountain, yet again, looked very steep. I knew I didn't have enough strength on my own to climb.

Eight weeks post-surgery (and back home in Ohio) I reread my journaled words from the first post-surgery time (3-4 years earlier) about "hope in healing." I needed desperately to hang onto that hope as I had been hanging onto God to get me through this and to figure out what my new purpose would be. I realized that I had written the same thing for my purpose back then, which was to share my faith and hope with others. I've been doing that through writing in a blog that started out as a way to keep friends informed of my progress while I was in Florida; it has turned into a ministry that many read and rely on every day. I am thankful for the means to serve and share. It was difficult to keep positive when recovery seemed so slow. It felt like crossing a bridge to find that "new normal" again. That second major healing season was again hard on me, and I had no idea it would be much, much longer than the first one. The infections lessened, so that was helpful and obviously the right approach – yet we didn't know it until we took the risk and stepped out in faith to where God was leading us. For months I struggled with eating (still softest foods three years later), digestion and bowel functioning. I didn't even leave home much. Once again I found myself right where I didn't want to be – "stuck in the mud," so to speak. I had told my family that there might be a point post-surgery when I wouldn't have the strength or desire to go on. I felt like I hit that point many times on the mountain, running out of patience and belief that the doctor felt things would eventually improve. I fought through discouragement and despair to look for God with my spiritual eyes. He reached out His hand and pulled me up again, offering the kind of encouragement and speculation that no one on earth could do. My faith friends were wonderful supporters, along with my family. Still, I often felt very alone. It seemed everyone else's life was busy, and life was going on without me. I used to be in the fast lane, and now I was just waiting, wondering when or if I'd return. I kept asking God how He could best use me since I was still here! His reply would be to rest and wait – and trust that He would work all things out for my good.

~

As I put the finishing touches on this book and update my condition over three years after the second major surgery, the bowels and eating have been painful, slow functions. They took a hard hit once again. Recovery has been yet another uphill climb. Patience has worn thin waiting for the stomach and bowels to adapt. Eating is yet again a challenge, and while some things have improved, I doubt I will ever be "normal" again. Normalcy had to be re-defined yet again. I get by, but typical functions of eating and eliminating should not be so difficult! It is a roller-coaster of up and down spells, good and bad days, and a mixture of all of the above. I try to hold onto hope that this particular function-path will regulate for good, but at best I might have to settle for good "seasons." I get small bowel obstructions often that I have to learn how to work through with massage/manipulation, exercise, medicine and wading through the pain. At times when the pain is so bad, my desire to live in this condition wanes. Heaven would be a much better option any time, but especially with the "no more pain or tears" promise. It is high maintenance just to find doctors who will deal with me. Since this is not a common problem, and the exact cause hard to pinpoint, few doctors know what to suggest. My husband and I tire of hearing "We don't know what to do to help you…" and become discouraged to even seek help. I look forward to good spells and appreciate them, trying not to fear another bad spell around the next bend. I have had to "health retire" from my teaching position, and it has been very hard to "lay down my trophies." I have to daily take up my cross and try not to question my purpose. Yet, God clearly tells me that He isn't done with me yet and plants in my heart and mind a desire to keep hoping. While I continue to be a strong advocate for my case and seek answers, I also realize that there might not be any. Meanwhile, I feel that God is calling me to serve Him through some care ministries and mentoring to others who are hurting. I try to lean on the Holy Spirit's guidance to hear what steps to take, knowing that even though I make plans it must be all in accordance with God's will. Therefore, if a connection or consultation does not feel God-directed or inspired, I try to just take a break from the quest for answers.

~

My latest search for answers came as a result of an inexplicable prompting by the Holy Spirit. There was such a strong pull that I cannot adequately explain it, yet I knew what I must do. I had applied for an evaluation at the main Mayo Clinic in Rochester, Minnesota, and within days of being granted an appointment one of my specialists in Ohio suggested the same place as a possible means of new testing and evaluation. I felt convicted by the Holy Spirit to go where He directed out of obedience. I didn't know why or by what means, but I knew to go. I started praying a circle around this trip and praising God ahead of it for how He would deliver on His promise. I knew better than to expect a cure or answer, but perhaps there would be some therapeutic measures or this would promote further research and help for someone else. I believe God had a purpose, because He always does – even when we can't see His plan. Even when our first scheduled trip was canceled due to a flight change on a stormy night, we knew God was in charge. It felt like a no… but it turned into a *not yet*. (Notice we often only see the first two letters "n-o.") We finally made that journey about six weeks later, having had to reschedule the entire trip. I started to question if I had misread God's direction to make this trip, but I was reminded that His timetable is not ours, and I would get there when it was meant to happen. The consultation was multi-faceted and took several days when it did occur. (In fact, a second trip with a continuation of consultations and testing needed to be scheduled even a few more weeks out. Then a third.) While an overall cause of the dysfunctional gastrointestinal situation was not found, physical therapy was recommended. Then the task was to find an offering closer to home, and my own research ensued. I was able to get some help on a much smaller scale than what I could have received at the Mayo Clinic, but it was within my own state and a reasonable driving distance and could last longer than a couple of weeks of treatment. Like most treatments, the therapy worked for a while, but the improvement in bowel functioning was hard to maintain on my own at home. But I took the relief while I could get it, and I feel that it opened some doors for this therapist to learn how to work on a patient with my complicated set of issues and be able to extend that experience to helping others. Meanwhile, symptoms of an overarching autoimmune issue (of which interstitial cystitis might be one piece of the puzzle) continue to surface, as well as challenges of the autonomic nervous system (which could be affecting digestive and bowel functioning). The challenge remains to find a doctor (or team) who can put the pieces of the puzzle together. I may or may not get some kind of resolution or help for my overall situation, but I continue to be an advocate for research and asking questions. It might not even help me in my lifetime, but I feel certain that any kind of information gained will be helpful for someone else down the road. That might even be one of my children or grandchildren, or someone I never know. One thing I know – God has a purpose in our suffering and pain – and I know that He will use all this for good. So I face the mountain one day at a time and tell this story as I keep on climbing so that God will be glorified and others will feel encouraged to keep on climbing when their own way gets steep. (It also seemed fitting that I submitted this work for publication the very same week that I returned to Mayo Clinic in Minnesota for continued consultation with the gastroenterologist and neurologist. There's always hope, and I truly believe that God honors perseverance!)

The Size of the Mountain – God is Enough to Climb Your Mountain

When the way is steep, I will look up to You.

Early in my writing of this journey I considered the title "Is God enough to climb this mountain?" I was inspired by author Horatio Spafford who penned questions like "When sorrow comes is God enough?" and "When life throws its worst at me is God enough?" based on experience of the tragic loss of his family. But he answered that question with the well-known hymn that he wrote in 1873 – It Is Well with My Soul. It is an expression of his deep anguish and grief, and while he didn't try to hide that, he also acknowledged that he used this pain to draw closer to God and move forward. This helped me to realize that I was looking at the size of the mountain, trying to see the end of the journey while I dealt with my grief and despair. I soon turned that question around to make the statement (and promise) that God is enough. **Jesus looked at them and said, "With man this is impossible, but with God all things are possible" Matthew 19:26 (ESV).** It's not the size of the mountain that is important…it's the size of our God. We must put our faith in Him to accomplish BIG things.

I've been to mountains, hiked small trails on them, and have even stood at the top of Pikes Peak (after a drive up), and they are certainly monumental structures. I can imagine standing at the bottom, looking up; but I can*not* imagine literally climbing one. If somehow I did complete that task, I can only imagine the sense of accomplishment to reach the top…but then despair to look up and realize there is another mountain straight ahead in my path. And who knows how many more beyond that? Is Heaven on the other side? Will I reach it? Praise, Jesus, yes, but we just don't know how far this chain of mountain climbs through life extends until we each reach that eternal goal. But God is bigger than the mountain that you or I stand on currently and the next one and the one after that…or however long we are here on this mountainous earth. I do not mean to minimize the size of the mountain struggle, but I do mean to maximize God's strength for the journey. I need the reminder and share it…that not only is God bigger than anything, but His grace is omnipotent. It is more than enough. **"My grace is sufficient for you" 2 Corinthians 12:9 (NIV).** He can handle any size of mountain that we think we are facing. God wants only what is good for us even though the world offers us painful times and steep mountains to climb. No matter the size, there's no mountain or problem too big for God to handle. **"These things I have spoken to you, that in Me you may have peace. In the world you will have tribulation; but be of good cheer, I have overcome the world" John 16:33 (NKJV).** God is bigger than any of our problems and holds all the solutions, His will, and His timing in His hands. He won't necessarily take away our trouble, but He will give us the grace to endure it and the peace that comes in that offering.

During the journey the mountain might look *too big*. In fact, it might appear huge! You might feel as though you are looking straight up at that tower that is in your path. But if you get too focused on the mountain it can gain power over you and become the center of your thoughts. Instead, focus on God's presence with you and it will bring you peace that only God can give to calm your heart. **"Be careful, keep calm, and don't be afraid. Do not lose heart" Isaiah 7:4 (NIV).** God can change our perspective to look at the situation through His eyes rather than our own. He might not change our circumstances but can change our perspective. Our mountain might not change, but we can change how we look at it. The Apostle Paul's statement in **Philippians 4:11** encourages us that the way we view our circumstances is more important than the circumstances themselves. He wrote: **"I have learned to be content whatever the circumstances" (NIV).** It takes a while to get to the point of actual contentment, but it is a state of satisfaction with your situation – realizing that only in God can you find ultimate joy and peace, that He is the source of true contentment because He never changes. **"Lo, I am with you always, even unto the end of the world" Matthew 28:20 (ASV).**

"Is God enough…

When I face a mountain?

When someone betrays me?

When someone I love uses words to hurt me?

When I need to forgive what seems unforgivable?

When I am not forgiven by another?

When a loved one dies?

When I feel all alone?

When I struggle with health? When there are no answers?

When I don't know if I can make it one more day, even take one more step?

When I am let down and disappointed in my life?

When I am paralyzed with self-doubt, fear or despair?

When I wonder what tomorrow will bring?

When I wonder what God's purpose is in all that is happening that I don't understand?

_____, *is God enough?*

The answer to all these questions (and any you can fill in the blank) is: <u>Yes, He is. God is enough.</u> **"My grace is sufficient for you, for my power is made perfect in weakness," 2 Corinthians 12:9 (NIV).**

I have had many junctures in my journey when I've asked that question, but my answer is always in turning the words around to reply, "God is enough." I repeat that promise to myself often. His arms are wider than the biggest hug I feel I ever need, or the hand that needs to take mine and lead me on and keep me going. He has the biggest shield and sword to strike down Satan's temptations of doubt, fear, guilt or despair. It takes a big faith in our big God, and I believe the constant breath of the Holy Spirit fanning the flame. I know that He will strengthen me for the task as long as I continue to lean on Him. **"The eyes of the Lord range throughout the earth to strengthen those whose hearts are fully committed to Him" 2 Chronicles 16:9 (NIV).** *May God's light shine through me as He uses my experiences and trials to encourage others.*

When life becomes more than you think you can handle, don't quit. And certainly don't believe the lie that God is not enough. Instead, ask yourself, "Is God enough for me? Then plant His Word deep in your heart so you'll always have the ready answer, that yes – He is. He is enough for me, and for you: **"And my God will meet all your needs according to His glorious riches in Christ Jesus" (Philippians 4:19 NIV).** God is enough. God is enough. *God, help me to stand up when I feel like I can't do it on my own and to know that You are enough.*

3

Seasons and Valleys – The Ups and Downs of a Mountain Climb

"Life is one mountain after the other." (Haitian Proverb)

Life is full of ups and downs, just like a mountain climb. Bad things happen, then things improve, then another affliction comes – the ups and downs. Even illnesses have good/bad seasons, ups and downs. There are times on the steep parts of the climb that we feel the ground is shaking beneath us. I think that God understands and that's when He summons others to uphold us – even when we look around and feel like we are on that mountainside alone. Physically, we are, but God is always there. If we call out from a mountainside, surely we will hear an echo bounce back – and that is God responding that He is there. It might seem very quiet and not as much as we want to hear for support or encouragement from others at that point, but God is there and His presence is sufficient. We are never alone, even when we feel like it. We can rest assured that God is the rope and anchor and therefore press on, never losing hope. **"Lead me to the Rock that is higher than I" Psalm 61:2b (NIV).** The bad times can last for a while, like a long winter season. With each one, we tend to adapt as it levels out just in time for a new one to begin. The next season can be better or worse but sometimes it is just helpful to have a change. Like a respite, or a plateau on the mountainside, it can be the calm before a storm, or a rainbow after a rainstorm. But with reliance on God we can know that He is with us no matter what. By His grace we can find peace in any situation. Sometimes that sense of peace takes a while to come, just like awaiting spring after a long winter. Yet we must hold onto the hope that is from Jesus and rest on His promises: **"For lo, I am with you always" Matthew 28:20.** Thankfully, **"The steadfast love of the Lord never ceases; His mercies never come to an end; they are new every morning" Lamentations 3:22-23 (ESV).**

After all, whatever happens is God's doing, for He is the arranger of *all* circumstances. While it is hard to be thankful for mountains, the ultimate trust is to say, *"Thy will be done, Lord."* He uses everything that happens to us to teach us, for it is all His doing. We are right where we are meant to be and in exactly the shape we are meant to be in…for a reason designed by God. Illness can take us to a place (or season of life) where we feel we are unable to do our life work, but we can still do God's work by using our situation and story as a witness for what He has done in our lives. After all, some of God's greatest workers are those who are physically unable to serve. Yet, we are all honored in God's sight. **"You are precious and honored in my sight" Isaiah 43:4 (NIV).** Then to honor God's will we must use that time to fulfill His purpose in our circumstances. *For such a time as this, I will speak of what God has done for me.*

We must trust in God's purpose even when the path is covered with thorns. I've heard that stepping over thorns builds our character while increasing our reliance on God. Like Paul, I try to thank God for afflictions that increase my relationship with God. He endured trial after trial, and the harder they got, the more he praised God and rejoiced. I wouldn't trade my closeness with God for anything, and if that means being in the valley…then I am thankful for those times on the mountain when I just cling to my Savior. It is easy to focus on our situation and tempting to grieve and complain. Instead, why not use that time to give witness for the One who gives us everything? God might be using that time to bring us to an awareness that only a valley will bring, or to strip us of all other distractions other than focusing on His Word. Instead of trying to get out of the valley, stop and drink from the cup you are served. **"Shall I not drink the cup the Father has given me?" John 18:11 (NIV).**

Jesus said this to Peter as he faced the officers of the Jews who were about to arrest him. He was fulfilling the Word as he knew what was about to take place. I think about how he knew what was to take place as He went to the cross, and often we wish we could see ahead…yet most of the time I think I'm glad I can't see what is coming. A mountain climber has an idea of the height of a mountain, yet s/he surely can't see the top while on the side. But something keeps the climber advancing toward the summit with a goal in mind. If God set me in this place and time, task in hand, then who am I to not take His direction? *Lord, life is not always easy, but I know that when I climb with You, it is always good. The harder the climb with its ups and downs, the more You are there. While I'm waiting, I will serve You. May everything I do point to You.*

Equipment – God is Light for Your Path

"The Lord is my strength and my shield" Psalm 28:7 (NIV).

"Your rod and your staff protect and comfort me" Psalm 23:4 (NLT).

Psalm 23 is a comforting scripture, often used during valley times. I recited it to both of my parents in their last days here on earth, knowing the words would be familiar and comforting to them. But I had never pulled out this one line – "Your rod and your staff, they comfort me" – to think about the tools that God provides in times of need. As our Shepherd, He provides His rod and staff. These could certainly be helpful tools on a mountain climb! God always sends His staff with His rod. A rod is usually thought of as a disciplinary tool, so perhaps in this context it is the affliction. A shepherd carries a staff as a walking stick (which would be an aid) and also to herd his sheep, so it is a tool of direction and guidance. I would conclude that this verse encourages us that God provides guidance no matter our circumstances. When He sends us up a mountain, we can be sure He will provide us with the equipment for travel. While surely there is a packing list of required equipment, our relationship with the Lord is the best tool for any journey. He will never send us on a journey without equipping us for what we need, even though we often think we know better what that should include. God is the only One who knows what we will encounter, so we need to consult Him in our packing! He will always send us forth with His staff, which He always provides with His rod. Actually, there are many scriptures that can serve as *walking sticks,* words and verses that can prop us up on our journey:

"He will have no fear of bad news; his heart is steadfast, trusting in the Lord" Psalm 112:7 (NIV).

"Weeping may stay for the night, but rejoicing comes in the morning" Psalm 30:5 (NIV).

"Your sandals shall be iron and bronze; as your days, so shall your strength be" Deuteronomy 33:25 (NKJV).

Jeremiah 29:11 is a perfect staff when the way is uncertain, better hope than any map could provide: **"For I know the plans I have for you and not to harm you, plans to give you hope and a future" (NIV).**

"Thou art the God that doest wonders; Thou hast declared thy strength among the people" Psalm 77:14 (KJV).

Whatever tools we take on our journeys, we must remember to keep our focus on God and our gaze upward. Sure, we have to watch our steps, but the best approach is to keep looking upward to God because He is always watching our steps and knows them before we even take them. **"It is God who will supply all your needs" Philippians. 4:19 (TLB).** Often in a journey we do not realize until a point much later down the path that God was carrying us all along, even when it felt like we were walking or climbing alone. While it is best to look forward, it is in our human nature to look back…but in that glimpse in the rear-view mirror it is often when we see how much He was carrying us and paving the way. Even if we get side-tracked and doubtful, we can turn quickly to see His face and know that He has been there all along, even though we sometimes don't realize it at the time. We must keep our eyes focused forward for **"His steadfast love endures forever" (Psalm 136:4 ESV).**

I truly believe that we understand the inner workings of our Savior best when we experience valleys and mountains, for in those times we have a deeper reliance on God. God's rod is like a schoolteacher pointing out a letter so a child will notice it. Martin Luther's wife once said that she would never have understood the practice of the Christian life and work, if God had never brought afflictions to her life. While it is difficult to be thankful for afflictions, God uses those dark times to grow our faith and a deeper reliance on Him. That is what Paul meant when he said: **"Whatever were gains to me I now consider loss for the sake of Christ. What is more, I consider everything a loss because of the surpassing worth of knowing Christ Jesus my Lord, for whose sake I have lost all things. I consider them rubbish, that I may gain Christ" Philippians 3:7-8 (NIV).**

We also need to put on our sturdy shoes for the uphill climb, knowing that we need a good sole and foundation: **"Thy shoes shall be iron and brass; and as thy days, so shall thy strength be" Deuteronomy 33:25 (NKJV).** This is also like putting on the full armor of God, which we should always carry into a battle. **Ephesians 6:11 "Put on the full armor of God so that you can take your stand against the Devil's schemes" (NIV).** Life can be a battle, and God never said it would be easy. He did not promise smooth sailing all the time. Even when things seem to be going "okay" it is best to have that stronghold in Jesus and a sturdy foundation for the journey. Just like when we set out on a vacation, we expect and hope for a smooth trip and a pleasant time. However, we never know what might happen, but with God in charge we know that we will never be alone or have to manage our circumstances on our own. **"Blessed are those who have learned to acclaim You, who walk in the light of Your presence, O Lord" Psalm 89:15 (NIV).**

Also we need to take along a *light* because the path will be dark at times. **Psalm 18:28 "You light a lamp for me. The Lord, my God, lights up my darkness" (NLT).** I wouldn't want to travel a mountain path alone in the daytime, let alone in the dark. But it's when the way seems darkest that God is the closest. Even in the dark, He is there. **Psalm 119:105** promises that God's word also provides **"a lamp to my feet and a light to my path" (ESV).** God's lamp is a better tool than the brightest lantern. He shines His light in the darkness like nothing else can. We need to allow God to hold our lantern and shine it in the direction that He wants us to go, even if it seems like a different pathway than we chose. For He promises that His light will continue to shine within us as we climb, keeping us from stumbling in the darkness. **John 8:12 "I am the light of the world. Whoever follows me will never walk in darkness, but will have the light of life" (ESV).** We wouldn't want to walk a dark pathway with just a little lamp. God provides the ultimate light, and His word shines light and gives direction. I can see where I'm going only because of God's light shining on my path and with Him leading the way.

If there is appropriate attire for mountain climbing, surely it is the full armor of God. That sounds like a Bingo "cover all" but we can't go wrong with the full attire approach. We never know what is around the next mountain bend. Life is full of battles on and off the mountain climb, but we are never alone in the fight. **"Be strong in the Lord and in His mighty power. Put on the full armor of God, so that you can take your stand against the devil's schemes" Ephesians 6:10-11 (NIV).** God gives us everything that we need, and our strength and power is from Him. We need to store it up to equip us for the mountain climbs. At those times an assurance in God's strength and presence is what we need to gird us for the journey. **"The Lord stood at my side and gave me strength" 2 Timothy 4:17 (NIV).**

Psalm 91 was a piece of God's armor, prayed over me as a shield of protection in my health battle. The words "deadly pestilence" seemed very appropriate when the infections were ravaging my body and threatening my life. We used God's word as a sword and leaned on the promises of truth therein this passage. By inserting my name for all the pronouns, it became a very personalized covenant of protection and refuge. I give God the glory for leading me to a doctor who could help me, and I know that ultimately all healing has and will continue to come from my Lord and Savior – my Refuge and my Strength. **"He who dwells in the shelter of the Most High will abide in the shadow of the Almighty. I will say to the Lord, 'My refuge and my fortress, My**

God, in whom I trust!' For it is He who delivers you from the snare of the trapper and from the deadly pestilence. He will cover you with His pinions, and under His wings you may seek refuge; His faithfulness is a shield and bulwark. You will not be afraid of the terror by night, or of the arrow that flies by day; of the pestilence that stalks in darkness…For He will give His angels charge concerning you, to guard you in all your ways. They will bear you up in their hands, that you do not strike your foot against a stone" (NASB).**

Above all the equipment, the best assurance for this journey is a steadfast faith and hope in Jesus. **"Apart from me you can do nothing" John 15:5 (NLT).** While it is natural to get caught up (or down deep in despair) in appointments, tests, information and all that comes with an illness, the best thing is to keep hope in God as Savior and Helper. A journey like this requires faith in the Great Physician and ultimate Healer. He is the one prescription that will provide the kind of strength and perseverance needed for the journey. He will **"…make you strong, firm and steadfast" 1 Peter 5:10 (NIV).** God's spirit living in and through me – that is all the equipment I need! Of course, the key to this connection is prayer. You've heard the saying "prayer can move mountains" – I don't know anything else as powerful to do that. Nothing is too big for God! **1 Thessalonians 5:17 "Pray without ceasing…" (ESV).** *Lord Jesus, help me to rest and let You carry my burdens. All of this life is too much to carry on my own, or even a little bit. Please do the heavy lifting and be my Guide.*

5

A Guide – He Will Carry You Up Your Mountain

"The Lord is my strength and my song" Exodus 15:2 (ESV).

Where is God when you find yourself on a mountain? Even though you feel alone at times, He is with you. Always. You never climb alone. God is the ultimate tour guide and constant companion. He gives strength to the weary, grace to endure, His Word to sustain us, and confidence that He is working all things out for our good. In fact, God's grace and love abound in deepest waters and steepest mountains. Thankfully there is a Shepherd who will guide us over even the steepest mountains and lead us to a better place. **"The Lord is my Shepherd, I shall not want. He makes me lie down in green pastures; He leads me beside still waters; He restores my soul. He guides me in paths of righteousness for his name's sake." Psalm 23:1-3 (ESV).** That's the kind of guide and shepherd I want! He is the only one who knows every step of the journey ahead.

Psalm 23 is such a familiar verse, yet we often speak or hear the words so routinely that we don't realize how much of a guide our Lord truly is. He is the Shepherd who goes after even the last lost sheep. He will never leave us or forsake us. What better *guide* could we have in life than the One who leads us beside the still waters and restores our souls? He guides us on the right paths. We nod in agreement to the many times we have felt that strength and comfort, yet when trouble surges up or we feel like we're at another dead-end or bend in the road, we naturally become fearful. I believe God understands this human reaction, but He wants us to know Him enough that we feel His call to come to Him. **"Come to me, all of you who are weary and carry heavy burdens, and I will give you rest" Matthew 11:28 (NLT).** It might not exactly feel like *rest*, but it is a reliance on the only One who can sustain us and get us through our journey. I know that the Lord is my shepherd who will lead me…but I'm not sure about feeling the "still waters" until I get to Heaven – but part of His comfort is a sense of peace that the world cannot offer. **"God**

is our refuge and strength, always ready to help in times of trouble" Psalm 46:1 (NLT). I do know that He will be with me, and I can only find my soul's real strength when I stay quietly by Him. **"In quietness and trust is your strength" Isaiah 30:15 (NIV).**

There has to be some kind of rope to tie you securely to the Guide. I wouldn't want to climb a mountain unattached to anyone or anything for safety and security. In fact, I want God as my reliable anchor. At times you need to be pulled along when you feel like you can't take the next step. I often feel *stuck* in my situation and not very hopeful. That is when I struggle to see anyone attached and pulling for me, but I know that God is always there and will never forsake me. That is the only way I can keep going. **"But if we <u>hope</u> for what we do not see, we eagerly wait for it with <u>perseverance</u>" Romans 8:25 (NKJV).** There are two strong words in that verse that have helped me to keep on going at the toughest times: hope and perseverance. It is hard to persevere when you feel like you're climbing up a mountain with heavy boots weighing you down, no end in sight, no answer, and no relief for the awful pain. This verse reminds me that there is no hope *but* God. Even when it doesn't seem like He is moving, He is the only sure HOPE to rely on through doubt and uncertainty. Even when God delays, He is still doing something – preparing us and maturing our strength to be of service. His tapestry plan is always taping shape. **"Show me the way in which I should walk and the thing I should do" Jeremiah 42:3 (AKJV).** *Lord, help me to see You and how You work even in the midst of trouble…and that You always have a plan. Help me to trust Your way and to stay in step with You.*

God is with me in the valley, on the mountainside, and even on the cliffs! As we find out from life experience and are reminded in the Bible, life will have trouble. **John 16:33 "In this world you will have tribulation. But take heart, for I have overcome the world!" (ESV)** He told us this to offer peace, which is often hard to find and feel in the midst of an affliction. But every time I found myself trying to direct my own path and work things out, when I'd get on my knees and cry out to God in desperation…He would remind me that He will work things out according to *His* will. Yet, He will not leave us alone to manage on our own. He hears our cries and knows our pain even before we feel it. **"Have mercy on me, O God! I look to you for protection. I will hide beneath the shadow of Your wings" Psalm 57:1 (NLT).**

Not only will God give us light for our pathway, He will breathe directions into our hearts if we listen. **"Your ears shall hear a word behind you saying, 'This is the way, walk in it.'" Isaiah 30:21 (ESV).** The world can be so noisy and direct us this way and that, even through what others have to say. We have a choice of whose words we listen to and follow. I think that we have to daily ask God to guide and direct and help us to hear Him speaking to us at all times, not just when the way is treacherous. **Psalm 25:4-5 "Show me your ways, Lord, teach me your paths. Guide me in Your truth and teach me, for You are God my Savior, and my hope is in you**

all day long" (NIV). Psalm 63:7-8 "Because You are my help, I sing in the shadow of Your wings, My soul clings to you; Your right hand upholds me" Psalm 63:7-8 (ESV).

We can trust that God knows the way, even when we feel like we don't know where we're going. That's when we must look for the Lord, our Helper. **John 10:14 "I am the Good Shepherd, and I know my sheep" (NIV).** While I would prefer to know where I'm going at all times, that often isn't the case in life. It is our human nature to want to feel like we are in control and have direction. When the mountain just looks like a steep, treacherous path, with a winding course and uncertain pathway…it's comforting to know that the Good Shepherd knows the way. It requires faith and trust to know that it only matters that He knows the way. When sheep are left without their shepherd, they are bewildered, confused, and scared. They don't know which way to go or where to go with no one to lead them. We can feel that way, too, without a Shepherd to lead us. It is not for a flock of sheep to know the pasture that the Shepherd has in mind. They just have to trust and follow Him and stay close to the One who knows the way. **"The Lord is the stronghold of my life; of whom shall I be afraid?" Psalm 27:1 (NIV).** When our way is full of uncertainty, we should neither look too far ahead or behind us, but instead try to focus on God who is right in front of us – our constant companion and guide. He equips us for anything that comes our way on our journey. **"I am with you and will watch over you wherever you go" Genesis 28:15 (NIV).**

Although the world promotes independence, a dependence on God is a sign of mature faith and a firm foundation. The events of this world and its tribulation may try to shake us, but a stronghold in Christ is the only sure way to withstand the test. **"Find rest, O my soul, in God alone; my hope comes from Him. He alone is my rock and my salvation; He is my fortress, I will not be shaken" Psalm 62:5-6 (NIV).** He promises to strengthen and uphold us with His **"victorious right hand" (from Isaiah 41:10 NLT).** Having God as your rock and firm foundation is a solid promise, for nothing else on earth could provide the refuge and strength that God does. **"I will hide in God, Who is my rock and my refuge. He is my shield and my salvation, my refuge and high tower" 2 Samuel 22:3 (TLB).**

While this all sounds simplistic and sensible while reading the words, I have to daily take up my cross and seek God as my guide. I do get down a lot, and the pain is just overwhelming at times. I have had so many times when I have just wanted to give up! Why is a life with so much pain worth living – when you can't really live? I cannot fathom how anyone can make this journey without God! Every time I get low, and when I look back up…there is God's word. He comforts me, even though physical pain persists. When the climb is steep with chronic illness or other long-lasting difficulty, we must get to the point where we quit praying for God to get us *out of* the circumstances, but to deliver us *through* them. We don't have to give up on hope of healing, but we need to focus on strength to endure, prevail and stand firm. As we pray *through* our experiences, we will grow through them. **"The Lord is good, a strong hold in the day of trouble; and He knoweth them that trust in Him" Nahum 1:7 (KJV).**

"Why art thou cast down, O my soul? And why are thou disquieted within me? Hope in God; for I shall yet praise Him, who is the health of my countenance, and my God" Psalm 43:5 (KJV). It goes back to **"the joy of the Lord is your strength" (from Nehemiah 8:10 NIV)** and the promise that **"Lo, I am with you always" (Matthew 28:20 NKJV).** As dark or hopeless as it might seem, God is with us. In fact, He is ahead of us and already there. On the days that are tough to get out of bed and keep going…remember with me – one step at a time with *my God* as my guide. He will carry me, providing the strength that I need. *At the toughest times, Lord, help me to endure, knowing that You are near. May You always be my strength.*

To take this a critical step further, when we can't see our way and wonder when the pain or trouble will end, we have to trust our Guide, our God and Savior, to work it all out. We want to take matters into our own hands, and waiting is frustrating. It is a challenge to trust and leave the outcome up to God. As He promises in **Isaiah 43:2-3**, when we come to a place we've never passed through before, God is always present to help us: **"When you pass through the waters, I will be with you; and when you pass through the rivers, they will not sweep over you. When you walk through the fire, you will not be burned; the flames will not set you ablaze. For I am the Lord, your God, the Holy One of Israel, your Savior" (NIV).** While on the mountain, we have to concentrate just on the step ahead. If it seems like the chasm is too wide, realize that He is the bridge builder. He will build it, and He will carry us over it. Climb the mountain one step at a time. God will always move us in a forward direction and give the needed strength to climb and endure the mountain. You could have no better guide. May God be the honored companion and guide on your mountain.

"Lord, I trust in You alone. Rescue me because you are the One who always makes things right. Answer quickly when I cry to you; bend low and hear my whispered plea. Be for me a great Rock of safety from my foes. Yes, you are my Rock and my Fortress; honor your name by leading me out of this peril. Pull me from the trap…for You alone are strong enough." Psalm 31:1-5 (TLB). *Lord, when the terrain of my path is rocky and steep, help me to hold your hand more tightly. Your hope and strength sustain me.*

Plans/Map – Climbing Your Mountain One Step at a Time with God

"In all your ways acknowledge Him,
and He will make your paths straight" Proverbs 3:6 (ESV).

Trust God to open up the way before you as you go. The One who goes ahead of you, opening up the way, is the same One who stays close and never lets go of your hand. God never tires of the climb or grows weary. We are not to despair in our circumstances but rely on His unending power and strength. He will carry us when we feel like we cannot take another step and show us the way. **"He gives power to the weak and strength to the powerless" Isaiah 40:29 (NLT).** The key is taking one step at a time, or your situation one day at a time. God knows the next step you need to take and will be there in it with you as long as you trust in and consult Him. He will point which path to take and straighten the winding way before you as no one else can. **"In all your ways acknowledge Him, and He will make your paths straight" Proverbs 3:6 (ESV).**

It occurred to me on a car trip with the family that we have multiple choices for directions. We can use the old-fashioned paper maps, follow someone's verbal directions of a tried and true route, or follow the modern navigational systems. Sometimes when we follow what seems easiest or most convenient – or our own way – it does not always turn out the best. Or if we stubbornly refuse to ask for directions! When God speaks to us and gives a direction, we must follow even when it doesn't seem the way that we thought we should go or how we thought we'd reach our destination. We must *be still* for God to speak, listen for His direction, and then continuously recheck our route through prayer and connection to His guidance. **"You will see your teacher with your own eyes. Your own ears will hear him. Right behind you a voice will say, 'This is the way you should go' whether to the right or to the left," Isaiah 30: 20-21 (NLT).**

We need to remember God's will on an arduous journey. Even when things seem to be going well in life, and we kind of coast on auto-pilot, we need to remember who is steering and live according to His will. It is when the going gets rough that we lean harder on God, it seems, and yet we worry if He knows where we're going! Deep within the Psalms are pleas to God to stay true to His Word despite our circumstances, despite how hard the climb becomes on our way: **Psalm 119:37 "Turn me away from wanting any other plan than yours. v 43: May I never forget your words; for they are my only hope. v 49, 50: Never forget your promises to me your servant, for they are my only hope. They give me strength in all my troubles" (TLB).**

God chooses some to make the journey up a mountain. If we play the hand we are dealt and try to hold our heads as high as possible even on such burdensome journeys, we can remember that our endurance is a testimony to others. Mountain climbers know how to best pray for other climbers, even those who are at the foot of the mountain and just starting out. I think of how many times I wanted to turn back or jump off my rocky path, but instead I persevered with God. As hard as it is on some days, I must be obedient to where God leads – even if it is up a steep mountain with cliffs and obstacles in the path. Boldness and carrying on one step at a time depends on the trusting confidence that God is with me and for me. We have to see God on the path before us through eyes of faith as He encourages us forth one step at a time. **"The Lord Himself goes <u>before</u> and will be <u>with</u> you; He will never leave you nor forsake you. Do not be afraid; do not be discouraged" Deuteronomy 31:8 (NIV).**

Remember that with God as your guide, the road leads Home (to Heaven), what should be our ultimate goal. I learn more all the time on my own journey that while I keep climbing to reach the summit – that the top is not actually the point of a health resolution or the top of the mountain. It is more about hanging onto the ultimate goal of how I'll spend eternity. I wouldn't want any other goal than my ultimate arrival Home with Jesus. I think that has to be our guide and map to keep making the journey with an affliction. Thankfully even at the toughest parts of the journey, God promises to be with us and hold our hand. **Isaiah 43:2-3 (TLB) "When you go through deep waters and great trouble, I will be with you. When you go through rivers of difficulty, you will not drown! When you walk through the fire of oppression, you will not be burned up – the flames will not consume you. For I am the Lord your God, your Savior, the Holy One of Israel."** This is also true for a mountain climb. The path will not consume you, nor any obstacles cause you to stumble…if you keep your hand in God's. He will carry you *through and over*, not down the mountain. **Psalm 46:1-3 (TLB) "God is our refuge and strength, a tested help in times of trouble. And so we need not fear even if…the mountains crumble into the sea. Let the oceans roar and foam; let the mountains tremble!"**

Fear is a natural part of dealing with a chronic illness. We do not know what tomorrow will bring, and sometimes we don't know if we even want to find out! I often hear God whispering two words to keep me going: *"Fear not!"* Like a map gives direction for a journey, God's word can equip us with the direction to turn. **Isaiah 41:10** is a powerful direction and encouragement verse: **"Fear not, for I am with you. Do not be dismayed, for I am your God. I will strengthen you; I will help you. I will uphold you with my victorious right hand" (NLT).** Fear is also a tool used by Satan to go after us when we are already weakened by pain and illness. We cannot give into it but instead hold on tightly to Jesus, not letting darkness win. God works in the dark as well as the light, and in the scariest times we need to only cling to Him more tightly. This is when our faith grows, as God honors our trust in Him. **"The Lord is my light and my salvation; whom shall I fear?" Psalm 27:1 (ESV). "When I feel afraid I will trust in You" Psalm 56:3 (NIV).**

I have repeated **Jeremiah 29:11** more than once, and here it comes again – a necessary verse in a chapter about God's plan. He had a plan for each of us from the beginning, and He has always known that it would include this mountainous path for some of us. I believe He knew that I could handle this journey because of His role in my life. While sometimes I wish He didn't have that much trust in me, I have to trust in His plan, that His will be done and fulfilled. **"For I know the plans I have for you; plans to prosper you…and give you a future and a hope" (NIV).**

We have to be cautious that we don't miss out on God's plans for us, especially if it is something unwelcome in our lives…in *our* plans. What if an opportunity is like the lion that came into David's path? **"And when there came a lion…" 1 Samuel 17:34 (ESV).** David surely didn't welcome the lion, but he defeated it, and later he was able to also defeat Goliath. If he had turned away or not used that opportunity, he would have missed what God had for him. It was an opportunity in disguise, and likewise, we can use afflictions such as health obstacles to do God's work. Every difficulty that comes our way can be an opportunity to serve God if it is received in the right way. That is a hard thing to do or see when you are hurting, but I believe it comes through time and healing of the heart, perhaps only after a time of being still and hearing God speak. We need to be careful not to ask God to take away something that He might be using to build His kingdom. *Lord, open our eyes to see You on our mountains.*

Prayer can provide the best map, just offering your honesty and need for God to Him and leaning on His direction. I used this prayer in tough days of healing: *God, help me to trust Your healing process, slow as it may seem at times, knowing that You don't expect more of me than I'm capable of, and that You carry me when I can't manage on my own. Help me get through what You call me to do here until I get there – Home. Please be my Guide and keep me in step with Your plan.*

The View – Finding Joy
in the Journey

Even when your path is rocky…you will find joy in the journey.

"Have I not commanded you? Be strong and courageous. Do not be afraid; do not be discouraged, for the Lord your God will be with you wherever you go" Joshua 1:9 (NIV).

The view of the journey while on a mountaintop could be amazing and/or frightening, likely a mixture of both feelings. There are times when we can't see where we're going if the mountain itself is obstructing our view, or perhaps what is around the next bend. But it is comforting to know that we are always *within God's view.* He never takes His eyes off of us. **"From His dwelling place He watches all who live on earth" Psalm 33:14 (NIV).** It is good to know that God goes with us wherever we are, that we are always in His view. We are never out of God's sight, and He keeps a close eye on everyone whose hope is in Him. I am actually writing this section while we are traveling in the mountains of West Virginia, and looking out over the view of the valleys below it reminds me that on the mountaintops, plateaus, valleys, or storms of life, we are always within God's view. Jesus reminded Peter: **"You are seeing things merely from a human point of view, not from God's" Matthew 16:23 (NLT).** It is hard to remember that God's view is omnipotent. We must celebrate His watchful eye. It is encouraging to know that through faith in Jesus we are a part of His amazing view every minute of every day. And He sees over the mountain as no one else possibly can.

The view also depends on our perspective. If we can look for God's grace in all circumstances and see His goodness shine through even in suffering, we can find joy. It is not a natural (or easy) reaction to approach suffering in this way. If we look through God's lens, we can see that all things come from God, whether we like them or not. He is working things out that we cannot see and must trust Him for the outcome. We often cannot even see the bigger picture until much further down the road, and certainly not at the beginning of a journey. Like the saying "You can't see the forest for the trees," in this case you can't view the mountain while you're on it – or what will come of it. **"For our present troubles are small and won't last very long. Yet they produce for us a glory that vastly outweighs them and will last forever! So we don't look at the troubles that we can see now; rather, we fix our gaze on things that cannot be seen" 2 Corinthians 4:17-18 (NLT).** Maybe the view is intended to be the lesson that I learn? There's always a lesson on a mountainside, as God always has a purpose. I know that souls are grown through struggles. *Lord, help me to see the intended view and use it for Your glory. Teach me and use me, knowing You always have a purpose and a plan.*

One of the greatest joys of a mountain climb has to be that not only am I in God's view at all times…but that He is right there with me. In fact, He goes *before* me. I cannot go anywhere beyond His presence! He is in the good times/places, the scary ones, and even the lonely ones. In fact, He knows my next steps and when (or if) I'll reach the mountaintop! **"Where can I go from your Spirit? Where can I flee from Your presence? If I go up to the heavens you are there; if I make my bed in the depths You are there. If I rise on wings of the dawn, if I settle on the far side of the sea, even there Your hand will guide me, Your right hand will hold me fast" Psalm 139:7-10 (NIV).** I love that reassurance that I cannot go anywhere outside of God's view and His presence!

The secret to finding joy in the journey is rejoicing in the Lord and praising Him…no matter what. It is difficult to *not* be anxious, but it is through focusing on Jesus that the joy and peace can be felt (and in the worst times that is the *only* way). The focus on God's presence can overshadow the problems and fears. His love does not fail like earthly help does. **"Rejoice in the Lord always. Let your gentleness be evident to all. The Lord is near. Do not be anxious about anything, but in everything, by prayer and petition, with thanksgiving, present your requests to God" Philippians 4:4-6 (NIV).** True joy can only be made complete in God – for it is in Him that we can experience true and lasting joy of the heavenly kind, not the earthy kind that comes and goes.

Lord, help me to keep my eyes on the hills before me – one at a time – and then it might not seem as steep as a mountain. Uplift my perspective so that I can see your love and grace from my view…and know that You are with me wherever I go.

Plateaus – Encouragement from the Mountain

"Two roads diverged in a wood, and I – I took the one less traveled by, and that has made all the difference." – Robert Frost

Sometimes we just need to pause and catch our breath, look back and see where we've been, and look ahead to our goal and where we are headed. We need to be reminded of the direction and plan that God has for us, because He always has one that is best for us. **"For I know the plans I have for you…plans to give you a future and a hope" Jeremiah 29:11 (NLT).** It is always easier to keep going when you know the way, but at times the direction isn't clear because with illness we can't always see very far ahead of the step we're on at the moment. Perhaps you are pausing on a plateau of your mountain because God is calling you to a time of rest, then **"Be still and know that I am God" Psalm 46:10 (ESV).** Take the time to bask in God's presence and feel Him holding you as you refresh yourself in His holy presence. There are always resting places along a hiking path, and especially when you're climbing a mountain! **"Wait for the Lord; be strong and take heart and wait for the Lord" Psalm 27:14 (NIV).** I don't know exactly what the Lord is doing, and I can't see very far ahead in this journey; but I don't have to know beyond this plateau where I stand and wait in His presence. I know that He is strengthening my heart, and there is no greater strength than to walk with God. **"The Lord is good to those who wait for Him, to the soul who seeks Him. It is good that one should wait quietly for the salvation of the Lord" Lamentations 3:25-26 (ESV).**

I share here a little "pep talk" that I often have to give to myself as I pause on a plateau: It's good to remember all that God has brought you through and that He will see His plan through to completion, even if it's not where you thought you were headed. (When you're thinking, "I didn't even sign up for this mountain climb at all!) Wouldn't it make most sense that the mountaintop would be the end goal when climbing a mountain? But what happens when you think you're near the summit, only to find that was an illusion and the way is much longer? Or what appeared to be the top was just a smaller peak and there's much more of the way to go? Perhaps it is in these times that it is best to not have that crystal ball image – that so often seems it would make our path more do-able if we could just know the exact ending point and time. Time and again in my healing process I thought I was surely about there, that the "end was in sight." By "the end" I mean the solution – the resolution to the problem and a return back to some kind of normalcy. Occasionally I would look back and wonder what life would have been like if I had taken a different route or made different decisions. But we don't get a "do-over" in that sense. So when we pause to take a breath, we should look at how far we've come and not how far we have yet to go. For only God knows the ending to each of our stories, and meanwhile He will supply the strength we need to keep on climbing to parts unknown until we reach the summit, all within His protection and guidance. We can be certain that He does know the way. I am thankful for the obstacles I've overcome and that God has kept me on His pathway even when I've been on the brink or ledge and wanted to give up. Look back briefly; be thankful for where you're at and how far you've come with God as your Guide; and try to keep your focus upward. Take one day at a time, assured that God is in control. Carry on Christian Soldier, onward and upward, remembering where you're headed! **"In Christ…the old life is gone; a new life has begun!" 2 Corinthians 5:15 (NLT).**

Watch for hope, even when you can't imagine that things could get any worse. Take a deep breath on the plateau and know that God has you where you are for a reason. **"When life is heavy and hard to take, go off by yourself. Enter the silence. Bow in prayer. Don't ask questions. Wait for hope to appear. Don't run from trouble. Take it full-face. The worst is never the worst" Lamentations 3:28-30 (MSG).** *Lord, please give me the faith to believe that You can bring good out of any situation, and that You will teach me through times of adversity and pain. I know there is a purpose and You are working all things for Your good.*

Cliffs – Life Can Be a Steep Climb

"If God sends us on strong paths, we are provided strong shoes." – Corrie ten Boom

I often picture myself clinging to Jesus on a ledge where I've struggled to understand the way things are going. Or when I think I can't hold on any longer. It seems analogous to what it must feel like to be on a cliff or ledge on a mountainside. Others try to encourage with sentiments like "just go one day at a time," "hang on," or "hang in there"…similar to all those terms that I use when people ask me how I'm doing. There is nowhere else to go when you are on a ledge, pushed to the brink or barely hanging on over the side by your fingertips. What if you just want to let go and then it will be all over? It doesn't seem worth the fight to *just hang on*…but no matter how close to the edge of the cliff He may lead you, never snatch the guiding reins from His hands. Even when it seems the darkest, He is helping you to hang on…to Him. Sometimes we are pushed to the brink before we are pulled back by hope. **"When darkness overtakes him, light will come bursting in…" Psalm 112:4 (TLB).** When I feel like I'm barely hanging on, I picture Jesus with His arms outstretched hanging onto me. The Holy Spirit breathes a cord of hope to hang on, connecting me to God. He will pull me up to where I need to be and not leave me dangling. I like to imagine that I am actually tethered to God – that I can't get too far and will be pulled back by His grace, love and strength. **"God will never let you down; He'll never let you be pushed past your limit; He'll always be there to help you come through it" 1 Corinthians 10:13 (MSG).** He is our anchor in life's storm and on the cliff. Even when our faith feels weak, if it's anchored in God's promises, He will help us to hold on safely. **Joshua 1:5 "I will be with you. I will never leave you nor forsake you" (NIV).**

If we don't grab onto God, we can easily be entrapped on that cliff and fall into the pit of despair and self-pity. It can pull us down the slippery slope of depression where darkness tries to take over. Our only hope is to reach out to Jesus, the true Light whose rays can shine on us at any depth of despair. By holding onto Jesus, we can be pulled up to where we feel safe and secure again in His grasp. That is when we realize that we are not living for ourselves and our situation anyway, but for what God wants us to do *for Him*. **"He lifted me out of the slimy pit, out of the mud and mire; He set my feet on a rock and gave me a firm place to stand. He put a new song in my mouth, a hymn of praise to our God. Many will see and fear the Lord and put their trust in Him" Psalm 40:2-3 (NIV).**

I have been pushed to a very dark, lonely place at times on this cliff of doubt and health uncertainty. I have felt literally pushed to the edge at times with unending pain and unanswered questions, and as a result have not felt much hope in the storm, rather emptiness and loss. But even Jesus went into the wilderness to pray and ask that the cup be taken from him…but that ultimately God's will be done. My hope is not in any tests or doctors' advice. It is only in Jesus. It often seems when on the brink of despair, God's word will breathe a bit of peace to pick me up. I know from the promise of scripture that His power shows up best in weak people: **"For when I am weak, then I am strong – the less I have, the more I depend on Him" 2 Corinthians 12:10 (TLB).** At times His light of hope comes bursting in, and other times we are given just enough light to see the step we are on and to take the next. God knows how much we need, and trust is what helps us to hang on for all we can. God's Word always offers light, especially with comforting verses such as **John 14:1: "Let not your heart be troubled. v18 – I will not abandon you…I will come to you. v27 – I am leaving you with a gift of peace of mind and heart…so don't be troubled or afraid" (TLB).** All of these are such peaceful and comforting words that pull me back from the edge – the only thing I feel keeps me from letting go and falling. That is a glimmer of light in the dark valley. It is a peace you can only understand if you've felt pushed to a ledge, and the kind that only God can offer. Nothing on earth comes close to this kind of comfort and saving.

Perhaps instead of feeling like we're dangling on a cliff, we need to acknowledge that we can't do it alone and be willing to climb onward only with God's help. But we must also humble ourselves to admit our weakness and receive the help of others. I struggled a lot with this, fighting the desire to be independent and keep up the attitude that everything was fine. I actually got tired of hearing others comment, "Well, you look great!" I know that people meant well, but they had no idea how much I was hurting on the inside. Not that we need to burden others with our condition and feelings of pain, but when someone offers to listen or help, allow them to enter into your situation. God sends help through the love and care of others who wish to walk alongside us and help us over the rough spots. They also help us to look at the positives and on the bright side of the situation, like the parts of the body that do function correctly! How often do we thank God for the intricate workings of our bodies that we take for granted. What an amazing God we have! We are **"fearfully and wonderfully made" (Psalm 139:14 NIV).** Even at times when it seems like God is not with us, He is there. I admit that at the very worst peaks of pain I even became a little angry with God, but he feels our pain and cries with us, and He can take our anger! When

I think of the pain He endured for us all, I am humbled into thankfulness for all that does work correctly, and I know that I am never alone. He promises that He will not leave us to suffer too long: **"And after you have suffered a little while, the God of all grace, who has called you to His eternal glory in Christ Jesus, will himself restore, confirm, strengthen and establish you" 1 Peter 5:10 (ESV).**

Do not grow weary in the battle, even though sometimes God gives us more than we feel we can handle…alone. But with God, we can climb mountains! He gives us the needed strength, hope and courage. **"I remain confident of this: I will see the goodness of the Lord in the land of the living. Wait for the Lord; be strong and take heart and wait for the Lord" Psalm 27:13-14 (NIV).** Faith helps us to hold on and prevail, even on the rocky cliffs. For it is in experiencing the cliffs that we better appreciate the mountaintops. We are to **"be thankful in all circumstances…" 1 Thessalonians 5:18 (NLT)**, whether on a cliff or a mountaintop. Just like a rainbow follows a storm, there is always joy and peace that comes with relying on God in all circumstances. *Lord, help me to find joy in my journey, even when I feel like I'm on a cliff and there's no end in sight! I know that You are holding me up through all the ups and downs of my journey. Help me to always find my hope and confidence in You.*

10

Obstacles – I Didn't Sign Up For This!

How did I get here?
"He is able to do immeasurably more than all we ask or imagine" Ephesians 3:20 (NIV).

How did I get here? I didn't sign up for this! Lord, get me off this mountain! There are times of loneliness and despair on a mountain, when the climb becomes really, really steep. These are moments when our minds are fixed on our troubles and we can't see past the obstacles in our path. We can get stuck in a negative focus. God asks us to give those obstacles to Him (and this sounds radical – but to actually thank Him for them!) and to put our focus on Him. The very things we see as obstacles in our path are the actual materials He is using to pave the way we need to go. We can trust that He will pave a smooth path for us, too. **"In all your ways remember Him. Then He will make your paths smooth and straight" Proverbs 3:6 (NIRV).** He put us on our mountain in the first place (not to place blame) but to realize that He did sign us up for our climb and also promised to equip us with the tools necessary to make it. He has been there before (and on a steeper mountain that we can't even imagine), and He will lead the way and walk with us. There is something we are going to learn on our climb that He intends to teach us that cannot be learned anywhere but on this particular mountain designed for us. Not that He wants us to suffer or stumble or fall, but He will sustain us by guiding the way. I would never of my own doing volunteer for this mountain, but on it I have to fully rely on God and nothing else. There will be obstacles thrown in my way, but God alone can steer me around and sometimes through them. **"If the Lord delights in a man's way, He makes his steps firm; though he stumble, he will not fall, for the Lord upholds him with His hand" Psalm 37:23-24 (NIV).** Thankfully God does not waver when I stumble and fall. His strength is as firm as the mountain peaks!

When there is a barrier in our pathway, it is hard to move forward. We try to see the resolution and get sidetracked by the difficulties. We want the barriers removed before we try to pass through them or even attempt to get around them. It seems safer to hold back than to try to move forward. But one direction God will always move us is forward, even if it feels like a standstill with obstacles too great. He sees around barriers with a different perspective than we do, and sees the direction of our path like no one else possibly can. Only with God's strength can we keep going and with the fuel of the indwelling Holy Spirit! **"For nothing will be impossible with God" Luke 1:37 (ESV).**

Ask God to separate out anything in your heart that is *not of Him* – especially despair, doubt, discouragement, bitterness, anger – weeds that can so easily creep in during time of illness and uncertainty. Instead, focus on what is of God, with an attitude that He is in control and will guard your heart. Pray the words of **Proverbs 4:23 (NIV): "Above all else, guard your heart, for everything you do flows from it."** To literally go one step further (definitely *one at a time*), I would propose to try to find joy in the journey and in the presence of God. I had to fall down a few times as I tripped over obstacles in my path, and learn to trust that He will open up the way before me and show me the next step and the next one after that. **"I will guide you along the best pathway for your life; I will advise you and watch over you" Psalm 32:8 (NLT).** He can help us to focus on hope and what is pure, with a virtuous attitude as we strive to be more like Him. **"Fix your thoughts on what is true, and honorable, and right, and pure, and lovely, and admirable. Think about things that are excellent and worthy of praise…Then the God of peace will be with you" Philippians 4:8-9 (NLT).**

It is too overwhelming while climbing a mountain to calculate when you will reach the summit or top, how exactly you will get there, and what lies beyond. These are stumbling blocks in your path – thorns, rocks, set-backs. We can get caught up with keeping our heads down and looking for obstacles, when what we need to do is look *up*. There we will find Jesus pointing in only one direction – up. Plus, how can we see the top of the mountain (our goal as a climber) if we don't look up? Remember that He is the guide, even carrying you at times when you are not sure-footed enough to take the next step. Even when it feels like you are climbing alone, your Guide is there alongside. **"I will lift up my eyes to the mountains – where does my help come from?" Psalm 121:1 (NIV).** *Lord, help me to look up and climb with You.*

I think a mountain climber even needs to take a different perspective on the pathway and view the mountain(s) as one hill at a time. A hill is smaller, not as steep, and thus it shrinks the goal a bit. But you are still climbing, and remember that you are never alone. Disease can be a huge obstacle, bringing with it a whole host of other problems such as side effects of medications, loss of relationships, the inability to work and resulting loss of income and purpose, and so forth. But it is often when we feel like we have nothing but despair that we realize that all we really need to have is faith in God and trust Him to carry us. **"We are hard pressed on every side, but not crushed; perplexed, but not in despair; persecuted, but not abandoned; struck down, but not destroyed" 2 Corinthians 4:8-9 (NIV).**

The mountain itself could be considered an obstacle. While in the midst of a climb, the mountain seems to be the focus. You've heard the advice to "keep your eye on the goal." But I was informed by another victim of disease that racecar drivers do not look at the wall, rather they steer toward open space. That open space represents hope. It has more potential than the size of the mountain in front of you. I think it's that way with a chronic illness – instead of bracing all the time for a deadly turn or the impact (of the wall), you have to concentrate on that open space. We grip onto fear like that driver would grip the steering wheel. Our situations can freeze us into despair and fear, leaving little room for hope. Fix your eyes on Jesus rather than on the wall or the mountain. **"Let us fix our eyes on Jesus, the author and perfecter of our faith...so that you will not grow weary and lose heart" Hebrews 12:23 (NIV).** The context of this passage is times of suffering and hardship when we are urged to cling to Jesus. That is the *only way* to buffer the obstacle of suffering.

Sometimes Satan tries to throw a wedge between us and God by bringing suffering or pain into our lives to try to separate us from Jesus. On a mountain climb, it can be those obstacles (and anger and despair that are close companions to suffering) that try to trip us. That is when we need to stand on God's promises and proclaim His steadfast love for us – His supreme sovereignty through all the steps of life, both good and bad. **"Just as the sufferings of Christ flow over into our lives, so also through Christ our comfort overflows" 2 Corinthians 1:5 (NIV).** That is the time to *pour it out*. One of the stories in the Bible is of Mary, who had been saving some expensive perfume and she poured it out on the Lord Jesus. It was Mary's priceless treasure and so it was up to her what to do with it. She could have kept it to herself, or left it on the shelf to gather dust or save it for a rainy day. I think that's how it works with the gifts that we hold as priceless – we can choose what to do with them. Why store treasures on a shelf, never to use them? God gave me a challenge in life, and I had a choice of what to do with it. I could store up the lessons from God, but so they will benefit more than me, I chose to write about my experience and share it with others. Mary broke open the vial of perfume and poured it out on the One who was worth it all and more. That is so much my goal – to pour out love and learning from my walk with God. And we'll give Him all the glory! Don't leave your love sealed, safe, or placed high on a shelf. If we give gratitude in the midst of hardship, we'll find it will be like pouring perfume on the Lord Himself. Don't wait to be Satan's prey to catch us in our weak times. Use them to glorify the Lord and magnify His love and grace with us at all times. It is at these times that we have a choice – to wallow in self-pity, bitterness and despair, or to try to find the good in the situation and use it for God's glory. The results of the latter are far-reaching, not only for ourselves but for our true purpose on earth – to bring others to know God.

Fear, despair, and loneliness are natural parts of a health journey that can be obstacles in our path. These ill feelings can be the result of misunderstanding on the part of onlookers, especially if they do not invest themselves in your life enough to know what is going on or how to walk alongside you. This can feel like rejection. But the world sees with a limited perspective and understanding, not as God knows us. **1 Samuel 16:7b "For the Lord sees not as man sees: man looks on the outward appearance, but the Lord looks on the heart" (ESV).** We might not be able to help others understand, but as long as we know that God is on our side and working for us, we can keep our focus on His presence and call upon Him to help us. **"In the day of my trouble I will call upon You, for You answer me" Psalm 86:7 (ESV).**

Weeds, thorns and rocks (analogous to fear, despair, loneliness) are just a few of the obstacles on a mountainous path. Satan will try to throw other stumbling blocks in our way to trip us. We must push Satan's obstacles out of our lives, and that is never accomplished just with pleading or requests. We only win battles after bloodshed and tears, but clinging to Him with unwavering faith through it all. **"I cling to You; Your strong right hand holds me securely" Psalm 63:8 (NLT).** Only with God as our Leader can we proclaim victory in His name and be triumphant in the battle, coming out on top when we realize that He will save us from defeat if we turn to Him and surrender only to His will. Healing can come in His name, and suffering is never pointless or without reason. His love and power must be displayed and at work within us, remembering that the battle actually belongs to Him anyway! So does the victory. With an illness, that doesn't necessarily mean a resolution of healed body – but of healing of the soul and knowing that our most important victory is yet to come. God is with us and will fight for us. There are no obstacles or barriers to God. **"Now to Him who is able to do immeasurably more than all we ask or imagine, according to His power that is at work within us, to Him be glory…for ever and ever! Amen!" Ephesians 3:20-21 (NIV).**

Lord, help me to ignore the weeds, thorns, rocks and stumbling blocks in my path while I climb with you. Help me to know that despite these obstacles, that You are always with me. **"We will not fear though the earth gives way, though the mountains be moved into the heart of the sea, though its waters roar and foam, though the mountains tremble at its swelling" Psalm 46:2-3 (ESV).**

Strength for the Journey – Just Keep Climbing, Just Keep Climbing

God's strength stands as firm as the mountain peaks!

God will use a weakness to strengthen a purpose. For in my weakness, I am strong. It is like an opening – an opportunity for strength to shine through. A weakness will turn into strength, and darkness will turn into light. **"My grace is all you need. My power works best in weakness" 2 Corinthians 12:9 (NLT).**

The battle is heavy and the forces of evil and warfare are great. It is hard to stand up against the storm without a heavy shield. It also takes great strength to hang onto those cliffs, or worse yet when you feel like you're dangling from a fraying rope! I do not feel incredibly strong, just perhaps strengthened enough to keep climbing. Therefore, I am strong only *in Jesus*. We never know what lies beyond the next mountain bend, but I know I cannot face any of it alone. Even though we take many precautions and make many preparations in life, God should be our ultimate refuge. He is my best source of strength because He has **"equipped me with strength for the battle" Psalm 18:39 (ESV).** I cannot find it within myself, but only through God's steady source and supply that He puts within me. God will infuse us with strength. As we lift our burdens to Him, He lifts our hearts in exchange. Plus He has what it takes to do the heavy lifting, especially when we feel weak. **"Let us lift up our hearts…unto God…" Lamentations 3:41 (NIV).**

There are so many good verses about strength that are like my ropes to hang onto as reminders of God's strength in my weakness:

"Be strong in the Lord and in His mighty power" Ephesians 6:10 (NIV).

"My health fails; my spirit droops, yet God remains! He is the strength of my heart; He is mine forever!" Psalm 73:26 (TLB).

"The Lord is my strength and my song" Exodus 15:2 (ESV).

"Look to the Lord and His strength; seek His face always" Psalm 105:4 and 1 Chronicles 16:11 (NIV).

"In quietness and trust is your strength" Isaiah 30:15 (NIV).

"I lift up my eyes to the hills…My help comes from the Lord, who made heaven and earth" Psalm 121:1-2 (NLT). That is such a peaceful verse and one that partly inspired the mountain metaphor of this book. I suppose if one is climbing a mountain, the best direction to look would be *up*, the direction in which you are heading. Looking up also happens to be the typical direction we think of when searching for God and the directional reference toward heaven. However – and this is good to know – God is all around us (not just up).

God's power in our lives is the solution to so many needs. We are weak, yet He is strong. **"For I can do everything God asks me to do with the help of Christ who gives me the strength and power" Philippians 4:13. (TLB).**

At our lowest points when we are completely drained, and we feel like all our resources are tapped out, God is our help – yes, especially in times of trouble. How do we know and feel that? The words of **Isaiah 40:29** assure us: "**He gives power to the weak and strength to the powerless (NLT).**" We don't even have to feel strong, knowing that we can place our hope and strength in Him. He is our spiritual power source and shelter in the storms of life. "**They that wait upon the Lord shall renew their strength. They shall mount up with wings like eagles, they shall run and not be weary; they shall walk and not faint" Isaiah 40:31 (TLB).** When I feel like I can't climb any further, I know that God goes on before me.

Do I have enough strength…even enough to hold on in the worst moments? Of my own resources, I do not. The resources of courage, strength and faith are gifts from God. They are not of me, but of God. He is bigger than all my needs. Thankfully I do not have to rely on my own limited supply. On the other hand, God is the god of limitless resources. My job is to trust Him. Do I have enough faith to trust? **Ephesians 2:8** assures that "**…even trusting is not of yourselves; it too is a gift from God" (TLB).** I believe that is grace. The steeper the mountain is, the greater that supply of grace.

Strength comes from the realization of how much God loves us. He loves us in the good times and the bad, and is especially with us in the difficult ones. There is evidence in scripture when Mary let Jesus know that her brother and His dear friend, Lazarus, was sick and had died. **John 11:34-36: They told Him, "Lord, come and see." <u>Then Jesus wept.</u> The people who were standing nearby said, "<u>See how much He loved him</u>" (NLT).** Then Jesus raised Lazarus from the dead and in **verse 40** told Martha who was in disbelief, **"Didn't I tell you that you would see God's glory <u>if you believe?</u>"** God cares enough to weep with us in our pain and sorrow. Sometimes pain just reduces me to tears, and while crying doesn't reduce the pain it does remind me that God hears our distress and weeps with us. He even feels our tears on His face! He smiles with us on the mountaintops and holds our hand in the valleys, rejoices with us and hurts with us. *Oh how He loves us! Lord, I thank You for that mercy and grace, that You love me through it all.*

12

Perseverance in the Darkness and Fog – *Through it All*

"The Lord will fight for you; you need only to be still" Exodus 14:14 (NIV).

"Since we are surrounded by such a great cloud of witnesses, let us throw off everything that hinders and the sin that so easily entangles, and let us run with perseverance the race marked out for us" Hebrews 12:1 (NIV). "I press on toward the goal to win the prize for which God has called me heavenward in Christ Jesus" Philippians 3:14 (NIV).

At the darkest points of our long journey we will feel stuck in our situation and not very hopeful. We will struggle to press on and persevere. There is no hope but God in these situations. Even when the way seems dark and hard to see, God is the only sure hope to rely on through that doubt and uncertainty. **"But if we hope for what we do not see, we eagerly wait for it with perseverance" Romans 8:25 (NKJV).** That hope/trust approach requires what I like to call a "God confidence" – the blessed assurance and deep reliance that He is with me and will see me through, to step forward in boldness and in His strength alone. For I know I cannot do it on my own. **"The Lord is my Helper; I will not be afraid," Hebrews 13:5 (ISV).**

Due to the height and thinner air at higher altitudes, there is often fog in a mountainous climate. Fog can cloud the climber's view and prevent seeing the pathway or what even the next step might be. This is when we must persevere, press on in the journey and take one step at a time, holding onto God's hand as our guide. No map or plan will help as the footing seems unsure and the climber doesn't know where the edge lies. In the fog only God can see where we're going as we climb. **"Do not be surprised at the painful trial you are suffering, as though something strange were happening to you. But rejoice that when you feel the most forsaken and lonely, God is near. He is in the darkest cloud. Forge ahead into the darkness without flinching, knowing that under the shelter of the cloud, God is waiting for you" 1 Peter 4:12-13 (NIV).**

"We must suffer many hardships to enter the kingdom of God" Acts 14:22 (NLT). Not that we welcome tribulation, but it is at those times of need that we can feel closest to God. He is always with us but particularly has a heart for those in need (when we feel the most forsaken). Yet we have to open our hearts to let Him in and make that connection. God promises that no matter how alone we might feel, He is never far from us. **"If I ride the wings of the morning, if I dwell by the farthest oceans, even there Your hand will guide me, and Your strength will support me" Psalm 139:8-9 (NLT).** This means that God is with us through it all – not just on even paths but also on the rocky ones; not just on the sunny, thankful days but on all days. God promises: *"Yes, even there…and through it all."*

How do we keep climbing the actual mountain when we cannot see the top in the fog? That is where faith and trust come into play. The path ahead might look complicated, and you wonder how you'll make it and find your way. But remember there is One who is always with you, holding you by your right hand and guiding you. Even if a fog is obscuring your view and you can only see a few steps in front of you, that will cause you to lean more on Jesus and allow His presence to guide you on the path just ahead of you. **"Yet I am always with You; You hold me by my right hand. You guide me with your counsel, and afterward you will take me into your glory" Psalm 73:23-24 (NIV).**

A mountain climb is a journey of faith. Even when you cannot see what is around the next turn or what lies ahead, continue on with trust in God, tracing His hand when you cannot see. Deep in the heart of such a journey with your eyes so focused on God and the fog otherwise surrounding you, this deep faith cuts you off from everything but God. You realize that He is all you need, when you realize that your faith is the only thing that will get you through it. Despite hopelessness in your situation, you have to keep your hold on Him. Take hold of God and do not let go. **"Faith is being certain… of what we do not see" Hebrews 11:1 (NIV).** God is God…through it all.

He is always there, even in the fog. Even when we feel so alone, we can persevere knowing God is with us. His love is constant and that is what faith is about: knowing that when you feel like you can't take the next step, but to go on ahead because God is with you every step of the way. A mountain climber could have many points in the road where s/he thinks, "I'm not going to make it." Somehow God steps in with the needed adrenaline to keep going. **"I cried out to God for help; I cried out to God to hear me. When I was in distress, I sought the Lord" Psalm 77:1-2 (NIV).** If we are open to it in prayer **(Psalm 46:10 "Be still and know that I am God" NIV)** we can hear/feel Him beckoning us forth to take the next step. That is when we come to know God best. When all the noise stops, and it's just you and God alone, there is a peace that carries you on and speaks to say, *"You can do this. I am here."* **"I know the Lord is always with me. I will not be shaken, for He is right beside me" Psalm 16:8 (NLT). "But as for me, I watch in hope for the Lord, I wait for God my Savior; my God will hear me" Micah 7:7 (NIV).**

Whether you turn to the right or to the left, your ears will hear a voice behind you, saying, "This is the way; walk in it" Isaiah 30:21 (NIV). As mentioned in my introduction, it is best to never climb alone and to listen for the "call back" – a summon and encouragement from others who have gone ahead of you in such a climb and can help you reach higher ground. As much as there might be those who walk alongside you in a journey, there are many times of loneliness. Tune your ears to Jesus and His presence; let the voice of the Holy Spirit work within you as the call back – to guide you as this verse suggests. When you have a close relationship with the Lord, you will feel a guiding presence always with you at each turn. In this way, you are also obedient to God by following His direction and the plans He has for you, even if you don't understand them or wouldn't have chosen this path. It also makes use of your affliction by giving God the glory in all things, so praise Him on the way! Amazingly it makes the road seem lighter with that unexplainable peace that only God can give.

Talk to God on your mountain. He will meet you there. In that stillness time, talk to Him and listen for His voice. **"Be ready in the morning, and then come up…Present yourself to me there on top of the mountain. No one is to come with you…" Exodus 34:2-3 (NIV).** God will see you through the fog and show you the way to persevere. Even when it feels like you can't move or continue on, God will provide the strength that you need. **"He will give you the strength to** endure" 2 Corinthians 1:7 (GNT). Even when you feel you are at your "wit's end" as the saying goes. (I heard my mother use that phrase when I was little and only realized recently in my deep exploration of scripture that the term is actually in the Bible!) The antidote is calling out to God. **Psalm 107:27-28: "They were at their wits' end. Then they cried out to the Lord in their trouble, and He brought them out of their distress" (NIV).** After all, He can calm the raging sea! **"What sort of man is this that even winds and sea obey him?" Matthew 8:27 (ESV).**

Perseverance has been a word of encouragement for me as I have climbed my mountain. It is not only a "big" word, but an action that requires great strength and integrity. In such cases, that kind of strength can only come from a strong belief in and reliance on God. The word itself means "a steadfastness in doing something despite difficulty" (dictionary.com). That is not anything that can be purchased or earned. It also has helpful side effects, for it produces character and hope – also needed for the journey. **"Suffering produces perseverance; and perseverance, character; and character, hope" Romans 5:3-4 (NIV).** God uses our challenges to produce perseverance. He honors our persistence as an act of obedience and trust.

Dear Lord, thank You for Your strong grace when my circumstances look bleak. In my weakness, I cry out in utter dependence on You. Please make Your power known to me. I can't see what You're doing for sure, God, but I trust You. Help me to know that even when fog dims my view, that You are there. Be my hope, my peace, and my strength. May I stand strong through the heat of difficulty.

13

Let God Lead the Way Across the Mountain – *Give Me Jesus*

"As the deer pants for streams of water, so my soul thirsts for God" Psalm 42:1-2 (NIV).

God is our refuge and strength, an ever-present help in trouble" Psalm 46:1 (NIV). You can make it across this mountain with God's help. Don't back down! Whatever part of your journey you are on, God is with you! He gives hope that is a mighty beckoning force for a steep climb – an anchor for your soul. **"We have this hope as an anchor for the soul, firm and secure" Hebrews 6:19 (NIV).**

Climbing a mountain brings us closer to God because it's on the mountain that we realize how much we need Him. Do we need and rely on Him as much on the good days? Do we better realize that He is all we need when we are alone on the mountain and realize He's all we have? I have learned through my mountain climb how much I need God and depend on Him. I know I couldn't have made it alone, and I know that I have never been alone. God is always with me. I would often just utter three words: "Give me Jesus" – like throwing out the anchor of my soul. It isn't a verse, but it's a life-phrase that I have come to use so much during my climb. It's a short, call out to God – a declaration that I need Him to lead me and don't want to do it any other way but with Him as my Guide.

God is always taking us on a path that will strengthen our faith and deepen our trust in Him. **"He knows the way that I take…" Job 23:10 (NIV).** But He leads us *through* trials and over mountains, not around them. Trials require us to lean solely on Him to lead us and to know that He is holding our hand all the way. We cannot rely on our own wisdom, understanding, or strength to take our next step. In our humanness we are too weak on our own, and especially if disease is ravaging the body! We have to trust that He is leading us, not daring to take one step alone. The best way to learn about faith is through a trial, as long as we rely on God to help us scale that mountain. **"With your help I can advance against a troop; with my god I can scale a wall" Psalm 18:29 (NIV).** God is honored to carry our burdens for us and is big enough to handle anything we can experience. His shoulders are broad enough to carry our problems and His hands strong enough to work out the details – not always the way we want but according to His plan. *Hold my hand and lead me through the trial, Lord.*

All that God requires is that we follow Him one step at a time. That is the *only* way to scale a mountain – one step at a time with God. It's easy to become anxious at the sight of the mountain looming in front of you; but know that God is leading all the time, even over mountainous terrain. If you take your mountains to the Lord and lay the worries at His feet, He carries the load for you. He equips you for the climb. In fact, He carries you. **"For He orders His angels to protect you wherever you go. They will steady you with their hands to keep you from stumbling against the rocks on the trail" Psalm 91:11-12 (TLB).** And He directs your path. **"Let your eyes look straight ahead; fix your gaze directly before you. Give careful thought to the paths for your feet and be steadfast in all your ways" Proverbs 4:25-26 (NIV).**

It is easier to linger at the foot than to climb the mountain. The steepness or the unknown can be discouraging, so we want to stay in the safety and peacefulness of the valley. But God has already climbed this mountain, and glory awaits us if we have the courage to ascend. God will move us forward when we are ready if we put our faith and trust in Him to guide us. He will never make us take even one step beyond what our feet are able to endure. **"Your own ears will hear Him. Right behind you a voice will say, 'This is the way you should go,' whether to the right or to the left" Isaiah 30:21 (NLT).** At times during the journey it will feel like a dead end – that there is no point in going on and there doesn't appear to be a way to turn – like a dead end road. Paul experienced many times when there appeared to be no way out, but he learned that when bad things happen they are opportunities for full reliance on the Lord. **"…that we might not rely on ourselves but on God" 2 Corinthians 1:9 (NIV).** When there appears to be a dead end, the only direction to look is up…to our Savior. He truly is the only way – **"I am the way and the truth and the life" John 14:6 (NIV).** *Give me Jesus!*

When facing a mountain (or while on it), it is easy to be filled with anxiety, especially of the unknown. It has to be one step at a time with God leading the way. As my journey continues, I can't be afraid of the future, but try to take down the safety chain of reservation and *let God.* I have to trust Him for the next step and not worry about what's around the next bend. My plans are not my own anyway, so really there isn't anything to *let go of* when we realize our plans rest in God's Hands. I'm glad He loves me so much to take the reins and lead me up (and down) the mountains. **"God arms me with strength, and He makes my way perfect. He makes me as surefooted as a deer, enabling me to stand on mountain heights" Psalm 18:33 (NLT).** God's voice of guidance and hand of steadiness gives me confidence to trust Him and climb onward. **"The Lord is my strength" (Exodus 15:2 NIV)** to go on.

God will supply all our needs, regardless of what we think we need or if we think we can't take one more step. **"And my God will meet all your needs according to the riches of His glory in Christ Jesus" Philippians 4:19 (NIV).** He knows our needs even better than we do! Our needs are prescribed by earthly standards, like a supply packing list for a trip or journey. But we can't pack for every circumstance or really know what all we'll need; only God knows that. Even though we have to prepare, it is best to remember and to trust that God really will supply all our needs. Nothing can ever separate us from His help if we stay focused and tuned into Him. If we stray or stumble, His grace pulls us back. He promises that we'll never climb alone. **"Nothing in all creation will ever be able to separate us from the love of God that is revealed in Christ Jesus our Lord" Romans 8:39 (NLT).**

Furthermore, God will guide us in darkness and in light, on crooked paths or ones that seem too steep to ascend. Even in the midst of pain there is always light shining into the darkness, reminding us that if we suffer with Him, we need never suffer without Him. **"If we suffer we shall also reign with Him" 2 Timothy 2:12 (KJV).** He directs our steps even when we don't feel like we can take another or even look up to see the way. The journey may seem impossible, but He will guide us and lead the way. He fully knows how hard our journeys are for us, and He goes on the path before us. They are never too hard for Him. **"I instruct you in the way of wisdom and lead you along straight paths" Proverbs 4:11 (NIV).**

We have to trust that God is leading us on the correct path even when it doesn't feel like it. Consider the story of the Israelites when God rolled back the sea and delivered them from the advancing Egyptian chariots. **"God did not lead them along the main road that leads through Philistine territory, even though that was the shortest route…God led them in a roundabout through the wilderness toward the Red Sea" Exodus 13:17-18 (NLT).** God showed them a unique way of escape by parting the water so that they could walk through on dry land. He created a pathway for them! I'm sure they wondered how they'd make it on such an unusual route, one they'd never dreamed possible! What if they had taken their own route or shortcut? It goes to show that when we feel like a way is not going to open up for us that God can make a way. It might not be the shortest or the one we'd choose to take, but with trust in His strength we must step onto it in faith. This promise in scripture reminds me that I don't have to know or understand the plan, only to know that God does and to trust Him: **"Trust in the Lord with all your heart and <u>lean not on your own understanding</u>. In all your ways submit to Him, and He will make your paths straight" Proverbs 3:5-6 (NIV).** God is omniscient and understands even when we do not. He creates open pathways where we see only obstacles and detours. Surely He can see us through anything! By faith I must seek His guidance in prayer and then trust and obey when I do not understand the direction. *Help me to trust, Lord, even when I do not understand.*

This is when confidence is needed and is a companion to faith/trust. I often coach myself with God's word of encouragement to step boldly. **Hebrews 4:16 "So let us come boldly to the very throne of God and stay there to receive His mercy and to find grace to help us in our times of need" (TLB).** My code words for this verse are *"Give me Jesus!"* He is the only One who understands and can lead in the way that I need to go. I know in confidence that He will be with me, no matter what. The Lord of compassion promises: **"Though the mountains be shaken and the hills be removed, yet my unfailing love for you will not be shaken nor my covenant of peace be removed" Isaiah 54:10 (NIV).**

Keep your eyes open and focus on the present journey, the next step in front of you. Trust that God will open the way before you, and enjoy His presence. When we seek God, He will be there, showing us the next step to take. Walk (or climb) by faith, not by sight, trusting God for each step. For our sight will scare us and eventually fail us; but our faith will guide us in the right path. **"For we walk by faith, not by sight" 2 Corinthians 5:7 (ESV).** *From where I stand on the mountain, it's hard to see where this is going. But God, I know You're already there. Help me to trust You and keep my hand in Yours as You lead the way. I trust that You will never let go of my hand. Give me more and more Jesus to keep climbing.*

14

Knowing God Deeper –
Be Still and Know

"Be still and know that I am God" Psalm 46:10 (NIV).

Times of pain and illness are ripe opportunities for realizing total dependence on God, when you fall on your knees (or lie curled up in pain) with your eyes focused intently on Him. You literally come face to face with God in a needy way and can discover who He is at a more intimate level. The world around you tends to blur when you are wrought with pain and yearn for some kind of peace that can't come with physical relief. This is the time to know God deeper and find that peace and comfort that He alone can give. **"You will keep him in perfect peace whose mind is stayed on You, because he trusts in You. Trust in the Lord forever, for the Lord God is an everlasting rock" Isaiah 26:3-4 (ESV).**

There are times in the journey when the climb seems to be at a standstill, kind of like being stuck in your tracks. We aren't moving forward, nor can we back down the mountain. While it is frustrating to wait on things to improve or something good to happen, God is likely using that time to teach and prune us for a special way of using us. When it feels like we are just idly waiting for God to do something, it feels like we are just wasting time! I am continuously reminded that we are not on our own schedules; that God's is the ultimate timetable that operates on a completely different perspective of time. But we have to wait in the right way and in a place where God can meet us. He is, in fact, waiting on us to meet Him – in order to strengthen us and establish our resources for how He wants to use us. I do believe He brings good out of all situations, even when we can't see it while on the mountainside. So this waiting requires patience, deep trust and obedience, especially when we find ourselves in a situation that we didn't plan on or would have ever chosen. God says **"Wait for it patiently" (Romans 8:25 NIV).**

Patience is not only a virtue, but I feel it requires the handiwork of God, like a miracle to help it to happen and to refine the skill. Just like a garden needs continual attention and pruning, the patience virtue needs to be weeded and tended to continuously. The garden of our hearts can get weedy and overgrown all too quickly! That is why we need to come to the garden often and bask in the Lord's presence. That is the only way that fruits of the Spirit (like patience) will grow. We are reminded repeatedly in God's word to be patient. **"Be still before the Lord and wait patiently for Him" Psalm 37:7 (NIV).** Some of the most productive things happen in our souls when we are being still and waiting on God. I have learned that when God asks us to be still, He is going to do something with that. **Psalm 46:10 "Be still and know that I am God" (NIV)** seems like a welcome and restful thing to do, but it has taken me over two years of inactivity from work to refine that skill, and I'm still working on it. Busy people would likely welcome time to just sit still, but it is a difficult activity to stay away from distractions and the noise of the world that clamors for our attention in many ways. It is a challenge to force a troubled spirit into quietness and rest along with an active body. In the beginning of my forced time period of stillness, I had trouble saying no and pulling myself away from some of my usual activities that I was trying to hang onto. I would use the excuse, "My spirit is willing, but my body is weak." I really was too weak at times, but soon I didn't even feel a willing spirit anymore, and eventually I repressed the temptation to feel guilty about that. It took a while to "get it" – what it meant to slow down and rest. It is a lonely time, too. But sometimes God will pull away all our dependencies so that we realize that He is our only "mainstay" – a term I like to use to refer to the One to whom we can always turn. When it seems like everyone else is going on with life without you, know that God is there – ready and waiting for you to rely on Him. When God pulls us in to know Him deeper, He demands our total attention and reliance. We are to focus on Him on that mountainside and rely on His guidance. It doesn't have to be a lonely journey if God is guiding. **"Taste and see that the Lord is good! " Psalm 34:8 (NIV). "Blessed is the one who takes refuge in Him! The Lord is close to those whose hearts are breaking…The good man does not escape all troubles – he has them too. But the Lord helps him in each and every one" Psalm 34: 18-19 (TLB).**

Times of health issues and rest afford time to spend alone with God and really focus on being still and knowing Him deeper. A focus on God also keeps us from negative thinking and too much dwelling on our situations. He can also do His best work when we sit in the stillness of His presence. Instead of picturing myself alone on a mountainside, I like to picture my hand in Jesus' hand, and then the climb is not as steep. He is my dwelling place, where I can hide and rest in the shadow of His almighty wing. **"He who dwells in the shelter of the Most High will abide in the shadow of the Almighty" Psalm 91:1 (ESV).** At these and all times, God is the most important and lasting relationship that we can ever have. Like all relationships, we have to work on this one with prayer and study of the Word, along with focused attempts to sit still in His presence. There is a special strength born out of solitude and time alone spent with God, and the purpose is that God is trying to pull us to a deeper place, to know Him better. He is calling us to another purpose and is going to use us in a mighty way – not necessarily the way that we had planned for ourselves. This is when *trust* must be our tool, and surely what the verse **"Walk by faith and not by sight" (2 Corinthians 5:7 ESV)** means. We can't see where it's all going, but God knows what He's doing. We don't need to know or understand…just to know God. **Psalm 91:2 (ESV) "I will say to the Lord, 'My refuge and my fortress, My God, in whom I trust!'"** *Lord, I love dwelling under the shadow of Your wing, and I long to be in Your enveloping presence. I never want to be anywhere else! I want to focus my attention on the One who never leaves my side!*

The words of **Romans 8:28** have always been a favorite scripture: **"God causes everything to work together for the good of those who love Him and are called according to His purpose for them" (NLT).** These words have an even deeper meaning to me now. As I look back over my journey to date, God has been working all things together, piece by piece. While I was waiting on Him to move and act and take care of me…He was doing all of that, just in His timeframe and not the one I wanted. He has been piecing all the circumstances together like in a tapestry that I can't yet see the total design. Each step has been part of a bigger plan, and I am thankful to know that I was chosen to be a witness for God with my life journey. The greatest call of all is to share your testimony and be a witness, even if it brings one person to believe in God. So all things are working for the good of those who love God **"…and are called according to His purpose"** even when it doesn't seem like it at the time. I think it is only in retrospect that we can see that happening with the limited perspective of our human eyes and minds. That is also trusting when we cannot see, the epitome of faith: **"Faith is being sure of what we hope for and certain of what we do not see" Hebrews 11:1 (NIV).**

God's love and truth is like a mighty mountain! He is unmoved by circumstances, obstacles, storms, anything. As hard as that rocky mountain feels and appears, God could crush it! His steadfastness is more stable than the toughest mountain. There is more of God to know where that came from! This is the part of **Psalm 46:10**, after learning to be still**…"and know that I am God"** – to know Him more fully. How do we do that?

There have been times during my journey when I have to shut out the world, the pain, and just bask in God's presence. I feel He uses these times for us to know Him at a deeper level and to just know that His grace is sufficient, and in Him we can do all things. **"I can do all things through Him who strengthens me" Philippians 4:13 (ESV).** Paul's secret in these words was finding contentment in his affliction, knowing the power of Christ in his life and letting that direct his path. He didn't like what was happening to him, but He knew that his relationship with God and knowing Him deeply was his source of strength and power. With a focus on God's presence, we can know that He is in all things, and we can go on with the strength that He provides. We can stand securely on the promises of God provided in His word that should be a part of getting to know Him more deeply. He reigns on that mountain and stands on His word, no matter how difficult the journey. **"How beautiful upon the mountains are the feet of Him who brings good news, who publishes peace, who brings good news of happiness…Our God reigns" Isaiah 52:7 (ESV).** That is encouragement to keep climbing when you feel you cannot go on any more.

The tasks in **Psalm 46:10** to **"be still"** and **"know God"** require great strength, but they result in what I feel is the highest attainment and greatest triumph of the Christian faith. In knowing God deeper, our understanding of well-known yet sometimes perplexing verses about grace and strength have more meaning and an incomprehensible sense of peace: **"My grace is sufficient for you" 2 Corinthians 12:9 (NIV).** This comfort offers a sense of *peace transcending understanding* – a phrase, a feeling, a sense that cannot be adequately explained with words or definition. It must be experienced. It is that feeling that you know that God has it all under control, even when you don't understand at all. You realize that you don't have to understand. That is another term that is tucked away in a familiar verse that we often turn to for comfort, and only the experience can bring it to have meaning:

"Do not be anxious about anything, but in every situation, by prayer and petition, with thanksgiving, present your requests to God. And <u>the peace of God, which transcends all understanding</u>, will guard your hearts and your minds in Christ Jesus" Philippians 4:6-7 (NIV). Peace doesn't always mean calmness or stillness, but more of an inner calm – a comfort in the storm – that can arise only through a heart firmly established in knowing God. It is then that you know that you know, despite the raging storm around you, that God is with you. His love is stronger and deeper than anything we could ever imagine or experience on earth. **"How long, how wide, how deep, and how high His love really is" Ephesians 3:18 (TLB).**

My journey with God has been a tough lesson with some rich learning outcomes. As a teacher I always say that there is nothing like a hands-on learning experience, which my journey has certainly been! I have learned a lot about grace and humility. **Ephesians 1:8-10 "God has showered down upon us the richness of His grace – for how well He understands us and knows what is best for us at all times" (TLB).** Sometimes it is hard to remember that God is in control and knows what is best for us and will cover us with His grace. But…how sweet to know and feel that in spite of difficulty, heartache or pain…God's love and grace covers us. That is *amazing grace* for sure. What I have learned about grace has, in turn, taught me about humility. I am not at all deserving of all that I have or even to still be climbing this mountain. I know that it is only by God's grace that I can tell this story and be used by Him. For that calling and purpose of service, I am greatly humbled. **"Humble yourselves, therefore, under God's mighty hand, that He may lift you up in due time" 1 Peter 5:6 (NIV).**

Above all the accomplishments in my life, knowing God deeply through my journey has been my greatest. (And it is always a work in progress.) When illness strips you of everything you did, especially your life work, you really need to hang onto a sense of purposefulness and integrity. While I have always wanted a close relationship with God, the period of rest and waiting has pushed me closer to that attainment through time for reflection and study as well on a deep reliance on God to keep going. This journey/climb has grown my prayer life to a greater level of intensity and earnestness. Storms will do that. So for that blessing, I am thankful for this affliction. **"Be joyful in hope, patient in affliction, faithful in prayer" Romans 12:12 (NIV).** I do not value anything above my relationship with God. Paul said that he considered everything he had accomplished worthless compared with knowing Christ: **"But all these things that I once thought very worthwhile – now I've thrown them all away so that I can put my trust and hope in Christ alone. Yes, everything else is worthless when compared with the priceless gain of knowing Christ Jesus my Lord" Philippians 3:7-8 (TLB).** God is good even when the path is covered with thorns. I've heard that stepping over thorns builds our character while increasing our reliance on God. Like Paul, I try to thank God for afflictions that increase my relationship with God. I wouldn't trade my closeness with God for anything; therefore, I am thankful for those times on the mountain cliffs when I just cling to my Savior. Faith is knowing that even when you don't understand what is happening and you're just barely hanging on, that God is your refuge and strength and you just sing of His praises while you hang on! I know that nothing can separate me from His love. **"I will sing of Your strength, in the morning I will sing of Your love; for You are my fortress, my refuge in times of trouble. You are my strength; I sing praise to You; You, God, are my fortress, my God on whom I can rely" Psalm 59:16-17 (NIV).** And what confidence this girds me with, to know that **"Nothing can ever separate us from God's love" Romans 8:38 (NLT).**

In other lessons learned through knowing God deeper (although in this case I feel like a bit of a slow learner)…God is increasing my trust skills and weakening my worry skills. I think that mothers are by nature worriers, but I am gradually getting better at turning my worries into prayers. Throughout my health journey I have realized that there is so much that I cannot control, that it pushes me to a deeper reliance on God's omnipotence and sovereignty. He is the One in charge and will lift the heaviness from my heart as I lean more heavily on Him. I believe we have to ask every day for God to help us to trust Him more and be reminded to lay down our burdens before Him. **"Therefore do not worry about tomorrow, for tomorrow will worry about itself. Each day has enough trouble of its own" Matthew 6:34 (NIV).**

Part of knowing God deeper and relying on Him as my Shepherd is to know and hear His voice. That comes with times of *being still and knowing God* (Psalm 46:10). **"He goes on ahead of them, and his sheep follow Him because they know his voice" John 10:4 (NIV).** As the sheep follow their shepherd and know his voice, I want to follow God and know His voice as He calls to me on the mountain path and guides me. When the light seems dim, that voice is the flashlight that we need. How scary to be in the dark and not have a light or sound to follow. **"Your word is a lamp to guide my feet and a light for my path" Psalm 119:105 (NLT).** Sometimes the sound of our Savior's voice will be the only guide that we have. Many times I have heard words or phrases – sometimes in the stillness of the night, or other times of solitude – and I know they come from the Holy Spirit speaking to me. They are brief words of encouragement to keep me climbing – like threads of Jesus' garment to hold onto and use for my journey. Some are words of comfort as if God is speaking, and some are words that I can whisper like "breath prayers" – quick calls right to Jesus. I have written these phrases in my prayer journal and repeat them and turn back to them often for strength:

Be still and know.

Fear not; I am with you.

I will never leave you.

I will direct your steps.

Stand firm. Wait patiently.

My peace I give.

You are a child of God. I love you.

Keep your eyes on Me. Trust Me in all things.

God is my strength.

I trust You, Jesus.

God is enough.

In Christ alone I place my trust.

Give me Jesus. (Sometimes it's just a matter of saying His sweet name. What a beautiful, comforting word!)

I am thankful that in my quest to know God deeper that He has sharpened my sense to hear Him speak, as well as given me a voice to share His words. *Help me to listen, hear, and recognize your voice, Lord, and immerse myself in your loving Presence. May all I hear and say and do point to You.*

15

Are We There Yet? – Healing on the Mountain

When I can't see the end of the tunnel, I will trust in You.

During a chronic illness we must adjust our thoughts about healing. Does it mean an end to suffering? A resolution to the illness? A period of remission? Chronic, after all, means persistent and ongoing with long-lasting effects. In that respect, will we ever complete this mountain climb? Will the suffering ever end? Are we there yet? **"How long, Lord? Will you forget me forever? How long will you hide your face from me?" Psalm 13:1 (NIV).**

I think up to one healing point in my journey I had been waiting on my mountain to change shape or disappear completely. Or perhaps I kept thinking I'd reach the top. But we have to keep moving forward with that goal in mind. We'd rather not face the mountain, but it is important to look up at the mountain ahead rather than in the mirror at ourselves. We can look in the mirror and focus on ourselves and only what we can see. Or, we can focus on the task before us and focus on God's will for us, knowing that He is working all things out and will be with us at each step. If this is the task He has laid before me, I must face it and remember that the battle and the climb belong to Him! As I keep climbing I do get closer to God, and I know that eventually I'll reach Home! *Lord, I keep climbing this mountain because I know it brings me closer to You!*

We must also consider Jesus' example of suffering during our own times of illness. He is our ultimate role model of how to handle any situation. Jesus did even ask that his cup be taken from him, but he obediently followed the path that God had laid before him. **"He learned obedience from what he suffered" Hebrews 5:8 (NIV).** How did he bear it? He did not give into despair, doubt and discouragement. He looked beyond the situation at the glory that was to come. He used his suffering for good, and he did it all for us.

The Bible is full of stories of Jesus' healings. Yet, not everyone gets healed physically. The only healing that is promised is of sin, since Jesus gave his life on the cross for our sin. So when we expect complete healing here on earth, we're mistakenly expecting what God has reserved for us in Heaven. God wants healing of our sins more than He wants to fix our bodies. God did not design us for comfort. Healing of the body on earth is temporary, but wholeness is eternal. Despite illness and suffering, God soothes the ailing body, the aching heart, and the weary soul. **"God heals the broken-hearted and binds up their wounds" Psalm 147:3 (NIV).** It is only by God's grace that we are healed.

There is always some form of healing going on, even if we can't see or feel it at the moment. God knows the bigger picture, even if the ultimate resolution is wholeness and healing when we get home to Heaven. Even Job, from whom much was taken, remarked **"Shall we receive only pleasant things from the hand of God and never anything unpleasant?" Job 2:10 (TLB).** It all comes from God. Thus, we must **"give thanks in all circumstances" 1 Thessalonians 5:18 (NIV).** I have realized that it is both the ups and downs that have given shape to my journey and written my story. Even when we struggle and can't see the end, God is always good.

A large part of healing is acceptance – not that we have to just sit back and take it, but to submit to our place in God's will, knowing that we are on a mountain for a reason. This acceptance requires a faith that the one and only Someone holds me and has the situation well under control. In essence, this is submission to God himself and His omnipotence. I have heard this directive (from Theodore Roosevelt) and ingrained it in my heart and mind for daily encouragement for the climb: "Do what you can, with what you have, (right) where you are." God will meet me there and equip me for the climb to which He has called me. God gives us strength and patience to endure even near-hopeless circumstances when we trust in Him. Through it all, He is strengthening me in trust and endurance. *May I always turn to You in trust, Lord, trusting only in Your care and provision for the climb.*

So it is that we look for moments of healing to keep us climbing and recognize that God is in all the details. Looking through a God lens heals our perspective and helps us to focus on hope. The mountain remains, but so does the strength of my God and the mountain belongs to Him. **"May the God of hope fill you with all joy and peace as you trust in Him, so that you may overflow with hope by the power of the Holy Spirit" Romans 15:13 (NIV).** *Thank You, Lord, even for my struggles – as opportunities to turn to You and seek Your face. Give me grace to wait patiently. When you cannot shield me from suffering, please give me Your unwavering strength to bear it and be at peace as I cling to You. I know that You will carry me through this life until You carry me Home to be with You in eternity.*

16

Blessings in Disguise – Blessings on the Mountain

"Whoever believes in me…streams of living water will flow from within him" John 7:38 (NIV).

Blessings aren't always obvious to us. Some are even overlooked. They might be so embedded within a situation that we can't see them until some point later. But they are always there, even if hidden. It takes time through some journeys to get to the point where you can call it a "blessing" – and the term "blessing in disguise" or "hidden blessing" seems quite appropriate here. Paul went through a lot of hardship and torment before he could get to the place where he said: **"That is**

why, for Christ's sake, I delight in weaknesses, in insults, in hardships, in persecutions, in difficulties. For when I am weak, then I am strong" 2 Corinthians 12:10 **(NIV).** It feels like a stretch to say that we delight in hardships or to actually feel blessed through a trial…but the blessing comes through getting to know Christ deeper through our sufferings. As Paul puts it, nothing else compares – that all is "worthless" compared to knowing Christ, that there is joy in suffering: **"Yes, everything else is worthless when compared with the infinite value of knowing Christ Jesus my Lord"** Philippians 3:8 **(NLT).**

What if these mountains of life were approached as blessings? We tend to delight only in what feel like positive "blessings" – *good* things that come our way. It's much easier to be thankful for those! A blessing, by definition, is God's favor and protection – "a favor or gift bestowed by God" (dictionary.com). So even our difficulties are gifts from God ("blessings"); but we often don't view them with thankful hearts. There is a blessedness that comes from a total flat-on-your-face reliance on God, and an intimacy in walking through the valley or on the mountain knowing that you need to hold onto His hand. Some days it's all in how you view what lies before you, and during a health journey a good perspective is imperative. Sure, you get tired of the climb, especially with no end in sight or just more of the steep mountain climb. That's when you need to try to view the mountain not as a whole, but one step at a time, thankful to just take another step. It's also helpful to sometimes consider not the summit of the mountain as the goal, but just the next step, the one right in front of you. Count each small step as a blessing instead of viewing the monumental, overwhelming task that lies before you. For as much as we don't understand in the midst of the climb, it is the troubles and difficulties that strengthen us, just as mountain climbing would strengthen the body. But this is true only if you are climbing *with God* to keep your steps sure-footed or even to totally carry you at times. Though we feel like we're climbing Mt. Trouble, God is in our midst, and we can't let the mountains intimidate us. God is greater than the sum of all the trouble in the world! He enables us not only to endure our mountains but to also grow stronger through climbing them. God's presence will be our strength. Even when we can't *feel* God's presence, we can *know* without a doubt that He is there. In the most difficult trials, God can bring the sweetest blessings. **"Though I walk in the midst of trouble, You will revive me; You will stretch out Your hand against the wrath of my enemies, and Your right hand will save me"** Psalm 138:7 **(NKJV).**

We are on a journey that leads to higher ground – not necessarily the summit of the mountain per se, but to eternity. **2 Corinthians 4:17-18: "For our light and momentary troubles are achieving for us an eternal glory that far outweighs them all. So we fix our eyes not on what is seen, but on what is unseen, since what is seen is temporary, but what is unseen is eternal" (NIV).** This is a good reminder that although the way may seem tough, we are just passers-by in this life. When we have the hope of Heaven as our eternal home, we can know that this is a temporary place and situation.

I recall prior to my last major surgery that I was ready to meet God face to face and actually longed at times to go there – go Home and leave this world and all the pain and troubles behind. I told my daughter that I was ready to see Jesus and if that is what happened during surgery, that I was ready and would run to him! She said that afterward I remarked (with some remorse), "Well, I didn't get to see Jesus." But in actuality I believe I did see and have seen Jesus throughout this journey – otherwise I might not have come so close! Kelsey had written in an update on my care/health blog at that time, "She loves the Lord so much and was disappointed she didn't get to see his face *yet*. God has one amazing plan for her here, don't you think?" **"For I know the plans I have for you…" (Jeremiah 29:11 NIV).**

As travelers on these mountains and in this life, we are to be thankful to God at all times. It is hard to be thankful for a problem in the midst of it, but we must thank God that He is with us through it and honor Him for that. There is always something that comes of a trial that we otherwise would have never experienced. **"Glorify ye the Lord in the fires" Isaiah 24:15 (KJV).** When we realize that even our most difficult paths are part of our journey, perhaps we can view them as stepping stones in God's shaping process. The climb is what actually refines our character and causes us to cling to God's promises with an even tighter grip. **1 Thessalonians 5:16-18: "Rejoice always, pray continually, give thanks in all circumstances; for this is God's will for you in Christ Jesus" (NIV).** How does one thank God for a disease? The verse does not say to thank Him necessarily *for* something, but *in* it. *Lord, I do not thank You <u>for</u> this disease, but I thank You in this state of being. May I use it <u>for</u> Your glory and to do work in Your great name! May others see You in my offering.*

I am actually thankful for affliction and suffering if it means I get to know Jesus more deeply. For it is in the mountain climb that I meet God there and know Him more deeply. That's what keeps me going on and climbing the mountain, thankful to even have a mountain to climb if it means I'll meet Jesus there. It causes my soul to long for God. **"As the deer longs for streams of water, so I long for you, O God" Psalm 42:1-2 (NLT).** We have to find joy in the journey, trusting that God is using all that we go through for His good. And the best blessing of all is that suffering leads to sharing in God's glory. **"If indeed we share in His sufferings, we may also share in His glory. I consider that our present sufferings are not worth comparing with the glory that will be revealed in us" Romans 8:17-18 (NIV).**

Lord, I know there are hidden blessings on this mountain climb. You are the Giver of all that I am and all that I have – including the illness and pain that I'd choose not to have of my own will. But I do thank You for the spiritual lessons embedded within my journey, as <u>Your</u> will is done. Help me to keep my eye on the ultimate goal and keep on climbing!

17

The Summit – I Will Praise You on the Mountaintop!

"Let the name of the Lord be praised both now and forevermore" Psalm 113:2 (NIV).

What actually is the summit of a metaphorical mountain journey? When and how does the climber reach the top of the mountain? Then is it the end of the journey or just the beginning? Is it a cure for the health affliction or healing in heaven? For me, the summit is not a cure, because a chronic illness is not necessarily resolved. Furthermore, in this case there is no earthly cure. For me, the summit will be Heaven where there is no more pain or illness. So I continue the journey because I want to reach Heaven! I am not Home yet, and when I get there how glorious it will be to not have pain and disease! And the clearest view of everything that happens will come when I reach Heaven's gates – the true summit of my mountain! So in the meanwhile, I'll keep climbing even when the mountain seems too high. God is always on it with me, and I know that Heaven *is* on the other side. **"I am with you and will watch over you wherever you go…" Genesis 28:15 (NIV).**

There has to be a breathtaking view from a mountaintop, and all that glory goes to God. Amidst the difficult climb of a mountain-climbing journey we must remember to take in the view and remember this is all the handiwork of God. Even though pain and suffering might be occurring all around, there is still the beauty and majesty that God created. Whether pouring out our heart in amazement or agony, it is all an offering to God. He wants to hear from us and wants us to talk to Him, but not just for our troubles but to also count our blessings. **"God is our refuge and strength, an ever-present help in trouble. Therefore we will not fear, though the earth give way and the mountains fall into the heart of the sea" Psalm 46:1-2 (NIV).**

Wherever God places us He does so to strengthen our faith, even if it's on a steep mountain. And I believe that He puts us there for a reason, and that comes with a special grace to sustain us and carry us through. If we can but trust Him even when we don't understand where we are, or why, He will carry us through with an unexplainable peace and joy. For God sees over the mountain as no one else can. After all, He never promised us an easy climb, just a safe arrival at the top. We can't, but God can see all the way to the top, the summit – which might be a very different view than what we would expect or imagine. But that is where the victory is, the time/place where there will be no more pain, and we will be whole forever. Healing and total restoration is not always experienced on earth, but it is a sure promise in Heaven. **"He will wipe away every tear from their eyes and there will be no more death or sorrow or crying or pain. All these things are gone forever" Revelation 21:4 (NLT).**

It is good to remember that this is not our home on earth, and this is not the end for believers in God. The true beginning is eternal life in heaven with Jesus. We're just lingering here on earth with our Lord, whether scaling a mountain or walking on level ground. Heaven is never far from those who linger on a mountain with their Lord. Instead of lamenting the entire journey, we must consider acceptance of what comes from God's hand and how to deal with it. It takes time, but part of the journey includes being able to say on the mountain: **"It is good for us to be here" Luke 9:33 (NIV).**

To this point the mountain has seemed like a large obstacle and a steep climb – a painful experience with a negative connotation. That's because climbing a mountain *is* difficult! But there's also those welcome "mountaintop experience" moments – times when we feel close to God. I'm sure reaching the summit of a mountain climb would feel like the latter – a positive, high-spirited experience that we wouldn't want to end! That's why I think that the summit just might be Heaven, rather than the ending of some difficult passage during our life on earth. That's all the more reason to want to keep climbing, if a mountain-top experience is even a taste of what eternal life in Heaven has in store. I'm sure I can't even imagine. Also, we can't often see how far we've come until we get to the point where we're on the mountaintop looking back on our journey. That doesn't have to occur at the end, but it is good to realize that throughout our whole climb (and whatever comes next) that God was (and will continue to be) with us. The summit signifies that God's ways are higher than ours, and He knows what is best for us. **"You do not realize now what I am doing, but later you will understand" John 13:7 (NIV).** Only from the mountaintop can we see how far we've come and realize all that God has done. Our troubles look a lot different from above than they do from below, when we are looking back instead of standing at the foot of the mountain, facing the steep and unknown climb. But we are never alone, at any point of the journey. *Lord, help me to praise You at all points of my journey, and keep beckoning me forward to the mountaintop! I keep climbing because I know You are there!*

I don't know what the rest of my journey on earth will be like. None of us do – except that we have a choice. We can choose to follow the world or choose to follow Jesus. I know that it is not an easy route, despite the countless blessings that we do experience on earth as well. For some the journey is also laden with illness or other heavy afflictions. I also know from experience that there is only one way for me to make this climb, with Jesus holding (or pulling) me by the hand. I know this life on earth is not my forever home, and sometime I will experience a sweet reunion with my loved ones and meet my Jesus in Heaven. **"I am hard pressed between the two. My desire is to depart and be with Christ, which is far better" Philippians 1:23 (ESV).** Like reaching the finish line of a race, it is good to have that goal or image of the mountaintop and to press on toward the triumph. **Hebrews 12:1 "…let us run with endurance the race God has set before us" (NLT).** Press on and keep climbing the race set before you, knowing that however difficult it becomes that God has your heart. Your prize is at the top of the mountain, when you finally reach Home – the eternal finish line.

For now, I will keep climbing with Jesus and praise Him on the mountain. I will search for His way in the midst of my circumstances. I will tell about my mountain and how I scaled it with my Lord. I know that when I reach the summit (which is really Heaven), I will place a flag of accomplishment there, wave a palm branch of praise, and proclaim the victory for the Lord. In the end our life goal should be to say as in **2 Timothy 4:6-7: "I have fought the good fight, I have finished the race, I have kept the faith" (NIV).** *Lord, I can't wait to dance with You on the mountaintop!*

18

It's not "THE END"...

"I have fought the good fight, I have finished the race, I have kept the faith" 2 Timothy 4:6-7 (NKJV).

Early in this journey I looked up at the steep mountain before me. I didn't want to climb. I wanted to stay at the bottom and sulk in despair. God begged me forward. *"I am Enough to climb; take My hand"* He beckoned me. I can't say that I immediately latched on and away we went without a care! It was a gradual agreement that I'd try, and that is where I feel the healing came. He waited at the foot of the mountain until I was ready to climb, and in retrospect, we had been climbing all along but He was doing all the work! I realize now that He was always with me and before me, paving the way, giving just enough light for each step. It became more about each step rather than reaching the top. The mountain didn't look so high; God leveled the climb. *Be still and know that I am Your God.* (Tough lessons that I had to keep working at and realize are parts of the lifelong journey.) *My rod and staff comfort you as I lead you beside still waters and steep mountains. I am with you…always. I am Enough. I am Your Strength. You never climb alone. I'm not finished with you yet!* Are we there yet? Where is *there*? The mountain doesn't look so high anymore, even though the climb feels painful at times. I no longer ask to be removed from the mountain if God is using it, only to be still and trust God to show me my next step. Or, help me be still in the step that I'm on and wait in His will. I know that He is always several steps ahead of me, always calling back with words of strength that I am to share, in turn, with others: **"Be strong and courageous! Do not be afraid or discouraged, for the Lord will personally go ahead of you. He will be with you; He will neither fail you nor abandon you" Deuteronomy 31:7-8 (NLT).**

When we're on a mountain climb, we have no idea what a long trek it might turn out to be. I thank God that I am still climbing, and still trusting, but I never would have chosen to be stuck in this place – on a mountainside. (I never signed up for a mountain climb!) But I have learned through my journey that our plans are not our own. We have to trust in God's plans for us and be obedient to where He leads. I am thankful, through it all, for my deeper trust and relationship with God. I believe it can only go this deep when you find that you are totally reliant on God to take each step and continue on where He leads, even if you can't see where you're going. When the rug is pulled out from under you, so to speak, and you fall flat on your back (more appropriately, on your knees), there is only one direction to look – up to the Savior. Seriously, there is no one else who will be with you and love you despite your condition and stick by you at the worst times. God is there all the time, even when everyone else around you seems to have gone on with their lives without you. Yet I have also learned that others' climbs can be steep for other reasons, even if they look smoother than mine. We all have our crosses to bear, but the only way I want to carry mine is with God's help in lifting the weight; for my experience will bring good to someone else if I use it to encourage them. God comforts us so that we can comfort others, thereby giving purpose to our suffering and bringing something good and positive out of it. As the Lord wraps His loving arms around us, we are to share that embrace with others **"with the comfort with which we are ourselves are comforted by God" 2 Corinthians 1:4 (ESV).**

As I look back now, and realize so much time has gone by and still here I am on this mountainside…I believe the journey is not so much about reaching a resolution, or ultimate healing (which I do believe could happen if it is God's will), as much as it is about the climb. It is about *whose* hand I hold on the journey. The climb continues, but so does the strength of my Savior. **"But as for me, it is good to be near God…" Psalm 73:28 (NIV).** The summit is not a pain-free, healthy, happy life on earth. It's about reaching an eternal Home in Heaven in the company of God and angels and relatives who have gone there already. Meanwhile, back on the mountainside, someone else is watching me take each step and how I handle it. I am hearing God tell me that there can be joy in the journey to just trust Him for the next step. I don't have to know it, or even the ending. Every story isn't a fairy tale, with the words "THE END." But I know where my end will be – Heaven, and instead of "the end" I want the closing words to be "Hallelujah! Amen!" That "end" will actually be only the beginning…

It is the climb that refines us. It is in the fire of affliction that tries to burn us, where we hang onto Jesus and trust Him, where we grow stronger in our faith. We can choose to feel sorry for ourselves at the worst times (which at times I certainly do get down), or to choose God. It is taking one day at a time with God leading the way. Many days when I awaken I have to say, "This day I choose God…" and acknowledge that this is the path He has chosen for me and the cross to bear. We need to be careful to not ask God to remove something from our lives that He might be using to build His kingdom. If we ask God to remove a little weight from our cross to make it lighter to carry…we might remove part of our journey that we need to do His work later on. If we ask God to change our story, we might not like the ending another story would bring! We never know how or for what God is preparing us. *This is our journey together, Lord, and I wouldn't climb it with anyone else but You! I know that You are with me every step.*

As I close this work that God has called me to do, I sit humbly at His feet. I cannot take credit for the words, as it is God's handiwork. He used me as a vessel through which to speak words of encouragement and hope to others. He has comforted me so that I could in turn comfort others and thereby share witness of Him. I am thankful for the opportunity to speak up for Him and to live every day for Him. From beginning to end of this book, the words have poured out by divine inspiration of the Holy Spirit. My part was to be obedient to God's call, submit to His will, and share my experience. Writing has been part of the healing process and a task that has taken me deeper in my relationship with and understanding of God….the reason I was called over and over to **"Be still and know that I am God"** from **Psalm 46:10 (NIV)**. As stated in **John 12:49, "For these are not my own ideas, but I have told you what the Father said to tell you" (TLB).** I want my very closing words to be a prescription for hope, a promise from the Bible we can count on at all times:

"Be strong and courageous, all you who put your hope in the Lord!" Psalm 31:24 (NLT).

My comfort kitty, Barney.
"Thy rod and Thy staff, they comfort me" Psalm 23:4 (KJV).

40 Days of Devotions from the Mountain

There are many "40" experiences in the Bible, most associated with times of hardship: God caused it to rain for 40 days and 40 nights; Moses wondered in the desert for 40 years; and most notably among many other examples, the 40 days between Jesus' Resurrection and Ascension. At one point in my journey after being inspired by a reading of Mark Batterson's (2012) <u>Draw the Circle: The 40 Day Prayer Challenge</u>, I prayed circles around my health situation and direction for my path for 40 days, including writing this book. Therefore, I felt it appropriate to include 40 days of devotionals taken from my health journal over three years leading up to publishing this book. The writing task has been a calling from God from the onset of my health blog right up to choosing a publisher and timetable for completion of my book. It is a work completed only through His power and by His strength. In Christ alone… Prayer and devotion has been a firm foundation for my **Psalm 46:10** quest to **"Be still and know…"** God deeper. Therefore, I felt called to make it a part of my writing and encouragement to others. If one person reads and comes to know God more deeply because of it, then the purpose has been fulfilled. May all this be for His glory…

(1) Fear Knocks; Faith Answers

When fear knocks, faith needs to answer. Fear keeps knocking at my door, and I'd love to say that I never try to answer on my own. But in my humanness, I head toward the door, reach for the handle, fearing the fear that is surely on the other side…and time and time again God intervenes. *(Thank God!)* I feel His hand on mine, opening the door for me, interceding on my behalf, facing the fear on the other side with a shield of faith. Sometimes I wonder who will get to the door first. I hesitate to let God take care of the circumstances, feeling I need to answer. It is always better to be cautious and to not react too quickly, kind of like letting a call go to voicemail. God is my answering machine and steps in and takes it for me with the reassuring message: **"Fear not, for I am with you always. Do not be dismayed. I am your God. I will strengthen you; I will help you; I will uphold you with my victorious right hand" Isaiah 41:10 (TLB).** I have learned from life experience that the less I react to fear and anxiety and let it go to God – giving Him space to handle the details – that I see through eyes of faith how God steps in and takes care of things. Nothing can separate me from my Savior's love – not even a door. *When I feel fear, Lord, help me to know that You are there.*

(2) In the Fire

"Be sure of this: I am with you always…"Matthew 28:20 (NLT). That is a critical reminder in the midst of trouble. Paul was reminded of that and worshipped God anyway from the prison cell. Daniel trusted in God's presence in the lion's den. Shadrach, Meshach and Abednego worshiped God in a blazing furnace. They were thrown in because they wouldn't bow down to King Nebuchadnezzar. But they never doubted God's ability to be with them, even as the flames grew hotter. They had so much faith in God and remembered His promise to be with them always… that they refused to follow the king's command and stayed true to God, their true King. Now THAT is trust! This health battle feels like an inferno, and the heat keeps increasing, becoming unbearable at times. But I know that God will remain with me, and I will forever praise Him through the fire. God often leads us *through* stuff, not around it. He will be with us *in* it. *"I am with you always"* doesn't mean just sometimes or in the good times; it's also (and might I say felt even more) in the dark, in the storms, in the fires. In the midst of the fire, if we keep our eyes of faith wide open we can see God face-to-face. He will meet us there. He longs to be our safe haven and refuge. God rescues us in so many different ways. I am so thankful that He is never hindered by our seemingly impossible situations. But we have to ask in faith and not confine Him to our limited resources and viewpoint. God is bigger than what seems like the most impossible situation to us. **"He is my strength and song in the heat of the battle" Psalm 118:14 (TLB).** *Lord, I don't know how this is going to turn out or what tomorrow will bring, but I know that through the fire You will be with me. Help me to remember this when my doctors are perplexed and don't know how to help me. Remind me that You are never stumped by what feels to me like an impossible situation.* Seek God in the midst of your fire, for He is enough.

"When you go through deep waters and great trouble, I will be with you. When you go through rivers of difficulty, you will not drown! When you walk through the fire of oppression, you will not be burned up – the flames will not consume you. For I am the Lord your God…" Isaiah 43:2-3 (TLB).

God's grace truly is all-sufficient. It's all we need. Sometimes in life when all of the worldly comforts are gone and all you are left with is pain and the world has nothing to offer but emptiness – God's grace is all you have. When you are stripped of everything, it is then that you realize that God's grace and love is all you really need. Paul learned firsthand that God's grace was enough. I give him credit for his effort in asking God three times to remove the thorn from his flesh: **"I was given a thorn in my flesh, a messenger from Satan to torment me. Three different times I pleaded with the Lord to take it away from me. But He said to me, 'My grace is sufficient for you, for my power is made perfect in weakness.' Therefore I will boast all the more gladly about my weaknesses, so that Christ's power may rest on me" 2 Corinthians 12:7-10 (NIV).**

Oh we might ask, but the thorn might not be removed. The only true healing we will ever experience is from God. In our weaknesses, He is drawing us near so we can heal in the truest sense of the word. We may not always heal in earthly (physical) terms, but we can always find healing in Christ. His power will work best in our weakness.

(3) Healing – In God's Timing

I long for healing. It is a slow process of restoration. Healing can feel as slow as watching grass grow or swimming in caramel! It's hard to see it happening or to feel any progress at all. It is easy to slip into an "I give up" mode during periods of suffering. But then I think about the misery that Job suffered through his afflictions and loss. That's when I have to ask the Lord to breathe patience into me. What makes affliction endurable is how God's sovereign mercy and goodness sustains us. Job, who suffered more than most, wrote: **"For to me to live is Christ and to die is gain" Philippians 1:21 (ESV).** It is up to God what portion of each we will endure. The healing portion is also up to Him. Our role is to trust Him and His timing and remember to thank Him *through it all* and look forward to His reward. Life might be full of brokenness and suffering, but Heaven will be more than gold and unimaginable gain.

Some get healing rather quickly, some get it eventually after enduring suffering and patience, and others not at all or in a form different than what they expected. Healing seems to be the prize that we long for and await during an illness. But we all get God's grace in the timing and form in which He knows that we need it. As we wait for healing, His presence and all-sufficient grace can sometimes feel like a consolation prize and the impatient recipient might feel like saying, "Gee, uh, thanks…is that all I get?" But that all is God's grace – often taken for granted as much as expecting our bodies to function properly. I often reflect on what a miracle it is that the complex digestive system actually works at all – with all the complex parts having to work in sync with one another in order to function properly. We take it for granted and expect it to work, not really thinking about its complexity until it does *not* work. The body is such an intricately-woven set of systems, and when one part doesn't function properly all the rest are affected as well. It acts like a domino effect. It really goes to show how much the body works as a whole. As much as we are **"fearfully and wonderfully made" (Psalm 139:14 NIV),** we need to be thankful each day that these bodies work and know that whatever glitches occur are still part of God's plan – and healing will take many forms to work all things together for our good. *Help me to wait in Your presence, Lord, with steadfast confidence that healing will come in Your way and timing.*

(4) Seasons – In all Things

Praise God who loves me enough to meet me in the valley and bring life and healing. Praise the One who provides the warm weather, the sunshine, the hope that comes with spring and new life, the quietness and peace of the snowfall…as well as seasons of pain and affliction that bring us to rely on God and know Him fully. **Ecclesiastes 3:1 "For everything there is a season, and a time for every purpose under heaven" (ASV)** has always been a favorite scripture, and with each season of my life and circumstance it offers a new shade of reasoning as I remember to trust in God's timing. No matter the season or situation of life, to Him be all the glory.

I have come to view this period of my life while dealing with the climax of health issues (and that finally brought me to laying down my teaching tools and entering "health retirement") as another season of life. It is a time of rest and healing. The rest effort had become my work (hard work), and the healing part has become a waiting period that is growing patience, trust and understanding in me. I don't know what healing might look like, and I have to work on these fruits of the Spirit every day…but I know that God is with me just as He is every season of my life. There is a scripture in Paul's letters that seems to be the way a Christ-follower should respond to such a season (or any) of life – without asking for miraculous deliverance from trouble but for gifts from the Holy Spirit of fortitude, patience, joy, and even the power to give thanks *in all things*. This should cover all seasons: **"May you be filled with His mighty glorious strength so that you can keep going no matter what happens – always full of the joy of the Lord, and always thankful…" Colossians 1:11-12 (TLB).**

(5) Celebrating Life

On my birthday I choose to celebrate life, knowing that from our first breath to our last – and every moment in between – that we are in God's care. **"The Spirit of God has made me, and the breath of the Almighty gives me life" Job 33:4 (ESV).** God made me just the way He wanted me on this very day. While it is not the way I would have chosen to be, nor am I often thankful for my body being this way…God paved this path for me, has pulled me out of the depths more than once, and for whatever reason has chosen to keep me around! I know that He has plans for me, even when I can't trace His hand. Although I have spent much time during the worst suffering season longing to be home in Heaven with Jesus, I am thankful on a birthday to celebrate God's gift of life and blessings. I recently read a good life question to ponder: *When plans are shattered, do our minds dwell on the circumstances or on the Lord?* While it's hard NOT to dwell on the problems and frustrations, I would much rather concentrate on Jesus. Plus with a focus on Him, our problems pale in comparison, and we are to honor and praise Him in all circumstances. **1 Thessalonians 5:18 "give thanks in <u>all</u> circumstances" (NIV)** – not just the good ones. I will choose to rejoice and praise God *anyway*…even when I am in pain or feeling unsure about the future. Chronic illness can rob one of joy and happiness…if we choose to let it. Life has many ways of robbing us of joy – but we can choose our attitude, perspective and approach. It goes back to that focus on God and how that keeps us centered on what is most important. **Isaiah 26:3-4** is an anchor for our souls in every storm of life and every day: **"You will keep Him in perfect peace, whose mind is stayed on You, because he trusts in You. Trust in the Lord forever, for the Lord God is an everlasting rock" (ESV).** Give me Jesus.

(6) Submission – I'm trying to surrender all, Lord

Sometimes we feel stuck in a place or situation where we would not choose to be…but God has each of us where He chooses us to be at that point in time for a reason. I'm battling with that notion as I try to accept having had to stop work (teaching) and be still. How and when should I adjust my life and purpose to this place? Am I wrong to question where God has placed me? I'm trying to consider what I can do in this season of stillness (besides rest) and consider acceptance if this is where God chooses to keep me for now. What is my purpose in all this? Sometimes it feels like I'm giving up, but it's actually more an act of acceptance and adjustment. In other words – submission to God's will. Surely Jesus felt this way…and then some! He knew what He had to do as he faced the cross but surely He wouldn't have chosen that path of his own accord. Not that my suffering has been anything comparable to Jesus' journey and sacrifice, I humbly add. Jesus was given over to God's will, yet he did ask if the cup could possibly be taken from him. **"Father, if You are willing, please take this cup of suffering away from me. Yet I want Your will to be done, not mine" Luke 22:42 (NLT).** Could there possibly be an alternative? He received a silent no. Surely if anybody ever deserved to have a prayer request answered it was Jesus! Yet he knew that the prophecy would be fulfilled. I don't blame Jesus for asking and know that I have approached the throne of grace with that same query for myself more than once. I guess it somehow makes me feel better to know that even Jesus wrestled with God's plan. He also provides the ultimate example of submitting to God's will. Have I asked God to take this cup from me? Yes. Have I wondered if this is a silent no? Yes. I know that God can move mountains if it be His will. I have to daily submit to His will and not being able to trace His hand in His plan for me. That requires a strong trust to know that He is steering, and I believe God is growing that fruit of the Spirit in me. It seems to me that a final act of submission could be called "surrender." How do we *surrender all*, as the good old hymn suggests? Lay it all on the altar and leave it there? Peter wrote that when Jesus submitted himself to the Cross, he **"left his case in the hands of God" (1 Peter 2:23 NLT).** I believe the key word is *left*. I give it over (so I think), take it back, give it over, take it back, etc. It's like a daily exercise cycle that we must push through because we know it is the right thing to do. It builds up our faith as we surrender to God's promise that He is working it all out for our good – the truth of **Romans 8:28** (another life verse): **"And we know that in**

all things God works for the good of those who love Him, who have been called according to His purpose" (NIV). God is omnipotent, always in control, and is always working everything into a pattern for good. Our part in the faith agreement is willingness to submit to God's will and plan – and then do something with it. I realize now in looking back that it has required a transformation from what *I want* to do and to what God has called me to do. And so I write, as I feel God has called me to do in this time of being still and waiting on Him. My task is to daily trust Him, take up my cross and follow, and continue my submission exercise – with God as my strength. *Lord, as I choose acceptance please grant me grace to sustain it, strength to stand firm, and the willpower to keep on prevailing.*

(7) Trying to Trust

I was reading in the Bible in the book of John about the wedding in Capernaum when Jesus turned the water into wine. As the story goes…when the wine supply was running low, Mary pleaded with Jesus to do something. His answer was something like, "I can't help you now. It isn't yet my time for miracles." (**John 2:4 NIV "Why do you involve me? My hour has not yet come."**) But then he turned water in six pots into wine, performing his first public miracle. Mary surely had not understood that Jesus' words really meant "My time has not yet come." She did not understand all that he was going to do later on; she just trusted him to help her at that moment of crisis. Here is the lesson from this story that hit home with me: *Those who believe in Jesus but run into situations they cannot understand must continue to trust that he will work in the best way.* When we bring our problems to Jesus we might think we know how he should take care of them. Yet he may have a completely different plan than what we have in mind. Like Mary, we should submit and allow God to deal with the problem as He sees best. Think of how when we don't see a solution we cry out in exasperation, "Help me, Lord! I cannot do this on my own!" How often do we think we know the solution and try it on our own…only falling on our knees when we cannot see the way out of the problem. We need to trust God in all things and rely on His control. He is always several steps ahead of us anyway and can see *way* beyond our scope of reasoning or view. **Proverbs 3:5 "Trust in the Lord with all your heart and lean not on your own understanding" (NIV).** Isn't it a relief to know that we don't have to know? God does. His grace and love covers us. *Thank you, Jesus!*

(8) Tools for the Journey: Thy Rod and Thy Staff and my Comfort Kitty

Psalm 23:4 "Thy rod and thy staff, they comfort me…" (KJV).

I never focused on this single sentence out of a very famous Psalm. I have used Psalm 23 many times and it is a common verse to use in times of loss and for comfort. I remember memorizing it when I was about ten years old in a religion class that was allowed to be taken in school at that time. But this one line of promise pulled out of the larger, familiar context stood out to me when thinking about the help that God gives us. "Thy rod and thy staff, they comfort me…" God offers His rod and staff as tools to comfort us. When God sends His rod, he sends His staff along with it. We often think of a rod for reprimanding, and often God uses a lesson to teach us – but along with it is always His staff, a symbol of guidance and gentle leadership. Aha – there is the *hook!* God always sends His staff along with His rod. I compare this to when the way is rough and the path is rocky (like climbing a mountain), God will provide us with the tools to climb. Sometimes the tools are sharp; others are of the more gentle form; both are needed and complement one another. He never promised an easy road but that He'd climb with us and equip us for the journey. Together, Thy rod and Thy staff, they comfort me. I guess they work well together as opposites (like my favorite odd couple, Ernie and Bert!)

Another gift from God that comforts me is my kitty, Barney. I truly believe that God sent him to me as a symbol of healing and comfort. In fact, I have called him my "healing kitty." It is a divine story how he came to me and in the timing. My daughter found him in Springfield, Ohio, where she was in college and was visiting the reservoir with a friend one day. Two kittens just appeared out of nowhere, as if abandoned (but I contend, sent by God), and they rescued them. She knew that I was missing our family cat (of 18 years!) which had just passed a few weeks earlier, and this was all right around the time of my last major surgery. I was facing a bigger mountain than I even realized at the time and would have many days when I'd rather just jump off than to keep climbing! Barney was a kitten, and he took to me right away when she got him to me. Even our vet has commented on our close connection, and as much as could be determined this kitten must have been born right around the time our old cat had died. That is a divine arrangement if I ever saw one! I do believe God knows what we need and when He can't remove our pain, will send us means of comfort to help us endure it, equipping us with tools for the journey. He knows how much I love cats and that I'd need a cuddly companion to love me through it all – a companion for my extensive days at home. I do believe in pet therapy and the emotional benefits of having a furry companion. I am thankful to God for the creature comforts that He gives us along with all the rest of His amazing creations. **"Every good and perfect gift is from above" James 1:17 (NIV).**

(9) Clinging / Jesus' garment is a security blanket

Often when people ask me how I am doing, I respond with "I'm hanging in there." What that means is hanging onto Jesus – or more appropriately, clinging to Him. The storms may come and the waters may rise, but I can have peace in knowing that Jesus will be with me. I cling to Him in faith that He will sustain me. **"Do not let your hearts be troubled and do not be afraid"**

(John 14:27 NIV) is a promise from the One who has never lied; the One who never lets us down. He is the One who is always on time and is prepared to help me face whatever comes my way on the journey. Fear tries over and over again to consume me, but that is Satan – for according to **1 Peter 5:8 "Satan prowls around like a roaring lion, looking for someone to devour" (NLT).** Satan tries to use suffering to diminish our faith, deceive us in our weakness, reduce us to doubt God's love and alienate us from Him. This is when I have to cling to Jesus all the more tightly, for I know that He will not abandon me. The earlier part of that verse in **John 14:27 says "Peace I leave with you; my peace I give you. I do not give to you as the world gives. Do not let your hearts be troubled and do not be afraid" (NIV).** As I cling to the hem of Jesus' garment (again, I visualize doing that and feeling that texture…), I feel a sense of peace that silences the doubt and fear. There is comfort in holding on, similar to the simplistic soothing of a security blanket. But when we hold onto Jesus it is a comfort and peace unlike anything the world can give. *Lord, help me to remember that when I feed my fears I lose sight of my connection to You. Instead, help me cling to You, feel Your peace, and to not be afraid.*

(10) Long + Suffering = Patience

God is never in a hurry, but He's always on time. Perhaps it's a good thing we cannot see His timetable. Surely it would not meet our approval or be what we would each choose. We have to remind ourselves when we're feeling frustrated and impatient for an answer that God is in control – and those are not just trite words – that He really does know what's best for us in all things. This includes what happens to us and the timetable. We often cannot see His hand weaving it all together until we look back on a situation. Like…you can't see progress on a project until you get something done! It is only when you pause (be still) and stand back to do a little progress check, that you can start to see how far you've come. This doesn't happen right away, but all worthwhile projects require patience. There is a good reminder in **Habukkuk 2:3 (TLB)** about patience: **"These things I plan won't happen right away. Slowly, steadily, surely, the time approaches when the vision will be fulfilled. If it seems slow, do not despair, for these things will surely come to pass. Just be patient! They will not be overdue a single day!"** Frankly, the word "just" in that passage grates on my nerves! It is *just* not easy to be patient! In fact, it's likely the hardest work I've ever done in my life – to be patient and wait on the Lord. I want to keep in control and handle things! I used to think I could do things on my own. Life experience and this climb has brought me to a realization that I do not hesitate to admit: I *cannot* do this on my own! Being still, waiting on the Lord, and trusting in His timetable is hard work – and I have to practice and exercise that skill daily. That is what trust in God is all about – and He provides the needed endurance. It's hardest when the pain and suffering is the worst – but that's also when we know that God must be our strength. <u>I am not strong enough on my own.</u>

I try to visualize actually placing my worries and burdens into God's almighty strong hands. The trick is letting it go and leaving it all there. Trust is knowing and believing that God can handle it. His hands are so much bigger than anything I could even place there. In turn, He hands me the needed perseverance and encouragement. There is unexplainable strength and peace in the shadow of His wing. **"He who dwells in the shelter of the Most High will abide in the shadow of the Almighty" Psalm 91:1 (ESV).** The thing that I must do is to believe that God can make a way even when there seems to be no way. There is a way out of near-hopeless circumstances. **"I can do all things through Him who strengthens me" Philippians 4:13 (ESV).** That is a promise that I can depend on, even when I don't see anything happening.

Longsuffering means "having or showing patience in spite of troubles" (dictionary.com) It is an appropriate term to apply to chronic health situations. It is actually one of the fruits of the Spirit that Paul mentions in **Galatians 5:22-23: "But the fruit of the Spirit is love, joy, peace, longsuffering, kindness, goodness, faithfulness, gentleness, self-control" (NKJV).** Some Bible versions translate it as *patience*. Either way, it is a beautiful virtue, and one that definitely requires experience and learning by doing, or on-the-job training. Longsuffering builds up a mature faith. Patience is one sign of that maturity, a quality that can develop through the passing of time. Think of it like a benefit – a positive side effect – of longsuffering. Trials of the chronic nature might seem endless to us, but God is timeless. He is never in a hurry like we tend to be. So while our souls wait upon the Lord, we pray for patience, perseverance, endurance, and even longsuffering – and know that God will use our situations for good. There is always a lesson on a mountainside, and souls are grown through seasons of longsuffering. **"My comfort in my suffering is this: Your promise preserves my life" Psalm 119:50 (NIV).**

(11) Get Real with God

"How long, O Lord? Will you forget me forever? How long will You hide Your face from me? Give me light in my darkness" Psalm 13:1-2 (NKJV). This is what David cried out when he was confused and thought God had forgotten him. There are times when we feel this same way: *How long must I suffer? Did you forget me?* When David later recalled what he knew – rather than what he feared – his sense of loss turned into a song of praise: **Psalm 31:1-6 (TLB) "Lord, I trust in You alone. Don't let my enemies defeat me. Rescue me because you are the God who always does what is right. Answer quickly when I cry to you; bend low and hear my whispered plea...For you alone are strong enough. Into your hand I commit my spirit."** David knew God's character, that He is always just and loving, even when it feels like we have suffered too long or feel forgotten. God knows our hearts and can take it when we cry out to Him in anguish. He longs to hear from us – for praises and for needs – and He can handle the complaints too! God wants us to engage with Him in our struggles, because He understands us like no one on earth can. He loves us so much that we can go to Him knowing that we have His fullest attention, as if at that moment God and I alone were the only two in existence. What a comfort to know Him so fully and to rely on Him, to wait on Him to act and move in our lives. That is what I consider a *stronghold*. God wants us to be honest, and to come boldly to the throne of grace. It's okay to plead with him and question…as long as we also continue to praise Him *anyway*, and *through it all*. But then I quickly wonder how I ever have the right to ask how long must I wait or suffer, to even question the will of God? Apparently David also quickly came to that thought after he popped the question, for soon in **Psalm 13:5** he followed up by proclaiming his reliance on God and acknowledgment that He alone was his strength: **"But I will always trust in you and in your mercy and shall rejoice in your salvation. I will sing to the Lord because He has blessed me so richly" (TLB).** David was very real in his prayers, and that is what a close relationship with God is all about. He is God, in the good times and the bad. He is with us *through it all.*

God knows the depth of our anguish and can see how long we've suffered. He is moved by our tears. That tells me how great God's compassion is and that He understands. **"Though He brings grief, He will show compassion, so great is His unfailing love" Lamentations 3:32 (NIV).** I am so thankful for that deep love that never fails.

(12) The Rewards of Serving / Blessed in Brokenness

Brokenness of any shape or form never feels like a blessing at first glance. It feels like a huge burden or a dark cloud looming overhead. But we can defeat those clouds/burdens when we pulse the heart of God and keep our focus on Him. In the lowest places and times of brokenness, a connectedness to Jesus makes all the difference. Sometimes we have to run toward our burdens and just deal with them, even when we'd rather run the other way. God is always at work, even in our brokenness. This is when His joy must be our strength. We have a choice to run (or fall down in an "I quit" fit!) or face the giant with God. My situation has stripped me of a lot, including my teaching and many things I would like to be doing. I miss teaching so much and feel like I was cut short on that service to which I was called. But in my brokenness, I know that I am still called to serve Him through worship and praise music. I believe that I was created to serve God. Even though it is hard to do it when I feel weak and weary in the battle, I want to continue to try to serve and speak of God's joy through my piano playing and praising with worship team at my church. It is my favorite form of worship and communication of thanksgiving to God. Above all my degrees and teaching experiences, what matters most is my relationship with Jesus and my commitment to serving God. I feel that I can serve God through my situation and speak encouragement to others, providing the example that we should praise Him *anyway*, regardless of our circumstances. **"Rejoice in that day and leap for joy, because great is your reward in**

Heaven" Luke 6:23 (NIV). I can only imagine how wonderful the reward of Heaven wiill be, but my reward now on earth is the closeness that I feel to God when I worship and praise. **"He is my strength and my song in the heat of the battle" Psalm 118:14 (TLB).** I believe that God uses everything that happens to us to shape us for service to Him. He longs to turn brokenness into beauty and use it for His good. So it is right to give Him thanks and praise and offer worship if I am equipped to do so and **"be thankful in all circumstances" 1 Thessalonians 5:18 (NLT).** We are also called to **"use every part of your body to give glory back to God" (1 Corinthians 6:20 TLB)** and to **"let them be a living and holy sacrifice...truly the way to worship Him" (Romans 12:1 TLB).** After all, we owe Him our lives! He would not give us abilities, gifts and life experiences unless He intended to use them for His glory. As long as I am able, and while I'm waiting, I will praise Him. I am too blessed to be broken!

(13) Sufficiency – How much is enough?

There are times in life when we've been pelted by tribulation, and we think we can't possibly take it anymore. We want to give up, but God says, *"Hold on; My grace is all you need."* How is that enough? And how much is enough? Wouldn't it be easier to do as Psalmist David did and long for wings to fly away? **"Oh, that I had wings like a dove! I would fly away and be at rest" Psalm 55:6 (ESV).** Yet even David knew that was idealistic and not reality, for soon he regained composure and claimed his stake in **Psalm 57:1 "My soul trusts in You; And in the shadow of your wings I will make my refuge, until these calamities have passed by" (NKJV).** I don't understand why I have this painful situation and must suffer, but I must trust in God's deliverance. I read over and over again about sufficiency and how Paul trusted that God was all that he needed. Paul asked God to take away what was causing him agonizing pain – the "thorn in his flesh." Then he asked God again. And again. Finally he heard Jesus himself speak to him. But what Jesus said was not what Paul wanted to hear, or what we want to hear when we plead with God in desperation. Jesus responded to Paul not by giving healing but by giving Himself: **"My grace is sufficient for you" 2 Corinthians 12:9 (NKJV).** His answer to Paul's pleading to take away the thorn was actually...no. But God wasn't just giving a flat "no." When God does not grant healing at the time we ask for it, what He does give is grace to endure the situation. I can imagine His response is something like, "Thank you for asking in faith; I'm sorry that the answer to your specific request is no...at this time; but here's what you need instead..." He will always provide what we need, even if it doesn't exactly match what we thought we needed. He is saying that He will be enough for whatever sorrow or pain we have and that He will strengthen us for it. His grace will be delivered to us in the form and quantity and timing in which we need it. He will give us the grace to endure the pain He does not take away. And I know with assurance that **"I can do everything God asks me to with the help of Christ who gives me the strength and power" Philippians 4:13 (TLB).** The worst spells of pain or trouble tempt us to ask in doubt

"Is God really enough? How much is enough?" But I've learned that the answer is in turning the words of that question around: <u>God is enough.</u> After all, I am not even worthy of all that God does give me, and who am I that He is even mindful of me? **"When I look at Your heavens, the work of Your fingers, the moon and the stars, which You have set in place, what is man that You are mindful of him, the son of man that You care for him?" Psalm 8:3-4 (ESV).** When put in that perspective, God's love and grace are *more* than enough. God will always give what we need the most, and it will always be sufficient. *Help me rely on Your word that Your grace is all I need as I ponder sufficiency.*

(14) A Blessing in Disguise

It's hard to think of pain as a blessing. What an oxymoron! If pain is a blessing, surely it is one in disguise. But my pain and health situation has passed through God's hand, so it must be somehow *for good*. It's all in what I do with it and how I allow it to draw me closer to God. I think my writing is my way of facing the battle and using it for good when I don't know what else to do for myself. It is a therapeutic way for me to deal with the pain. I feel it is God's directive for me to **"be still and know" (Psalm 46:10 NIV)** – that is, to know Him more fully. By writing about my faith, it is a way to face the battle and do something to benefit God's kingdom when I feel otherwise helpless. This is my offering. Even though I don't feel very strong in my pain, I know that God only chooses the strongest to be His warriors. I have been hand-picked for God's army, and I must be obedient to the call. Besides, others are watching how I respond! **"God who began the good work within you will keep right on helping you grow in His grace until His task within you is finally finished on that day when Christ Jesus returns" Philippians 1:6 (TLB).** Writing during the battle helps me to face my feelings and to be straightforward and "real" with God. I trust that the foundation of Jesus in my writing will keep Satan behind enemy lines. The writing becomes the blessing, disguised in a health battle. It gives a purpose and an uplifted perspective to the situation, pulling a blessing out of a burden. *To God be the glory in all circumstances.*

As I turn my focus deeper onto God, it helps to take my mind and eyes off of my painful circumstances. The story of Job gives attention to the character of God and discourages despair while encouraging hope. Even after all the adversity and loss that Job suffered, he asked, **"Shall we indeed accept good from God, and shall we not accept adversity?" Job 2:10 (NKJV).** Talk about looking for the blessings! Even when others questioned his circumstances before God, Job vowed, **"Though He slay me, yet will I trust Him" Job 13:15 (NKJV).** Job's affection for God didn't depend on a solution to his problems – a situation to which I can relate (with the puzzlement of my health situation and no ready solutions). He loved and trusted God because of all that He is: **"God is wise in heart and mighty in strength" Job 9:4 (NKJV).** Our love for God must not be based solely on His blessings or our circumstances day to day, but instead on the solid and reliable fact of WHO He is – our Rock and Redeemer. *God, please give me a right heart. Keep forefront in my mind and heart a perspective that helps me see the blessings that You have given me more clearly than my troubles. Lord, help me climb this mountain with and for You.*

(15) The Phoenix

Around the time of the fourth anniversary of my first ostomy surgery (7-3-07) I read in the Osotomy Association newsletter (yes, there is one…) that adjusting to having an ostomy is similar to going through a grieving process. It is an adaptation to a new way of life, and it typically takes some victims a year or two to actually adjust to an altered body. (Definition of an ostomy, by the way, according to the UOAA – United Ostomy Associations of America – is a surgically created opening in the body for the discharge of body wastes. There are three main types – colostomy, ileostomy, and urostomy. Mine is the urostomy, which diverts urine away from the diseased bladder.) Anyway, I was thinking back over the past few years of my own timeline and adjustment period. It was definitely a roller-coaster and a process with stages. It was similar to a grieving process in that I had to basically grieve the loss of a normal, natural body function and adapt to a new way of life. Plus, to date I have been through two rounds of this form of major surgery, and just as I was adapting to what I thought was the end of one mountain climb, I had to start up the mountain all over again! I experienced similar mountains in the actual grieving process when I lost my mother and then five years later my father. It's the analogy of the Haitian proverb that *life is one mountain after the other.* So true. But it is only possible to face one day at a time, one step at a time, with Jesus as Guide. One of my daily favorite verses is **Hebrews 12:2 (TLB) "Keep your eyes on Jesus, our leader and instructor."**

The symbol of the UOAA is the phoenix – which is a mythical bird that was raised from the flames after it died. It is a long-lived bird that is cyclically regenerated or reborn. Associated with the sun, a phoenix obtains new life by arising from the ashes of its predecessor (Wikipedia). People with ostomies are supposed to be "raised from the ashes of disease." The ostomy support group that I attended a few times would claim that you don't have to like your ostomy, but you do have to live with it – and those who say "I could never live with one of those…" don't live. That is a startling statement and realization. The ostomy is actually a lifeline and what saves us from the disease that was otherwise causing a problem or would have taken a life. The body part that wasn't functioning correctly is actually regenerated via the ostomy. I guess the Phoenix is a good symbol in that it gives life and shelter under God's mighty wing. **"He will cover you with his feathers. He will shelter you with His wings" Psalm 91:4 (NLT).** In this respect we must be thankful, for even this**.** Therefore, it causes me to turn my grieving into thankfulness that there is a solution to such problems. All things come from God, the Creator of life and the giver of all knowledge and gifts. I say it again and again…and may I say it until my final breath: **1**

Thessalonians 5:16-18: "Rejoice always, pray continually, give thanks in all circumstances; for this is God's will for you in Christ Jesus" (NIV).

(16) Cracked Pots

Paul says that as believers we are clay pots, meant to hold priceless treasure through the course of our lives. That impossibly valuable treasure is actually **"the light of the knowledge of the glory of God in the face of Christ" 2 Corinthians 4:6 (ESV).** We are called to display it. That is, we are to show the light of God in all we do and say. So if our very life purpose is to display the treasure of God, then wouldn't it shine more brightly through a pot that had chips and cracks in it where the light can shine through? It is through the test and the fire that the radiant glory of Jesus shines through to the wondering eyes of the world. There's always someone watching to see how we respond to a situation. It's like a shoebox container that houses a new pair of shoes. The box gets discarded just like our earthly bodies (vessels) do when we have no more need or purpose on earth. It is what we do with what was inside the box that is remembered. Jesus can shine through us despite the shape of our boxes. He is sovereign God who dictates what kind of box or pot to store His treasure in us. The more brokenness and holes we have, the more His light can shine through us. The more problems we have, the more God can use us. God will give purpose to our circumstances and use us in service and dedication to live for Him. *Lord, help me to allow You to finish my story and use my cracked pot all for Your glory.*

(17) Still Trying to Be Still

I have been trying to bask in God's presence. This helps to keep a positive focus, whereas it is too easy to be negative if the focus is on the health problem and a longing for an answer. God's love is more clearly revealed when the focus is on Him. Jesus has been calling me for quite some time to **"Be still and know…" (Psalm 46:10 NIV)** – with that message and scripture popping up everywhere. Being still is not an easy thing to do, especially for a person who loves to be busy. God is sure trying to grow patience in me. *Being still* helps me to focus on God and also sharpens the hearing sense for His voice to speak into my heart. It has helped me to find joy and be thankful for the part of this affliction that has taken me to a deeper place with God, and I always – as long as I live – want to have that quest to know Him more and to share what I learn with others. I have been circling back in my journaling to see how God has been at work through me in my writing. I saw a pattern of the theme in my journal words, with certain phrases and words repeated. Some are questions I repeat to God, others are words that I feel God is speaking to me. *Keep your eyes on Me. Ask, seek, knock. Change my heart, O God. Trust Him in all things. Obedience. Where do you want me to go and do? What is Your will? Focus on Me.* It makes me wonder how much Jesus has been calling me during times of busyness and I didn't hear him all these years! Was He trying to get my attention? Maybe "be still and know" could be translated to "shut up and listen"? I think we need to get quiet and still before the Lord in order to let Him do His work in us. He is growing patience in us as we learn to be still and wait on His timing. Focusing on God's presence overshadows all my problems and fears…even so far as bringing me to thank God for trials because they keep me closer to Him by relying on His love that never fails. **"Rejoice in the Lord always. Let your gentleness be evident to all. The Lord is near. Do not be anxious about anything, but in every situation, by prayer and petition, with thanksgiving, present your requests to God"** Philippians 4:4-6 (NIV). *Lord, help me stay near to You and focus on Your presence.*

(18) He Hears Me

I wrote this verse more than once in my journal, knowing that God is trying to use it to teach me: **"But as for me, I watch in hope for the Lord, I wait for God my Savior; my God will hear me"** Micah 7:7 (NIV). God has a pattern in the work He is doing in me: *be still, listen, wait, watch in hope.* This is all hard work, but these are clearly instructions from the Lord. But there is also a promise in that verse. When things don't work out or answers are delayed it is a reminder that God has it all under control and in His timeframe. *He hears me.* He will take care of those who call upon His name and believe in His mercy and grace. Sometimes it doesn't feel like He hears my pleas for an answer or for help, but that doesn't mean my pain is not felt or my cries are ignored. In fact, as soon as a prayer is sent up to God, an answer is already being formed. My part to play is to *watch in hope.* I continue to struggle with pain, and my stomach doesn't do well with food, but I know that God hears my cries for help and will sustain me. When I am not spared the pain, He gives me grace to endure it and hope to persevere. While I'm waiting, I will serve Him as best as I can and always give Him the glory. I watch in hope; He hears me.

(19) Go Forward; Stepping out of the Boat

"I lift up my eyes to the hills" (Psalm 121:1 ESV) and go forward. There is no other way around this mountain and no mountain too high for God! This verse is encouragement to keep climbing this mountain and going forward. It is also a fitting verse for my mountain book theme. Another metaphor for dealing with illness is getting out of the boat and having faith to walk on the water because Jesus is right there holding my hand. Peter did have a little faith, even in the midst of his doubts, to reach out and take Jesus' hand and step out of the boat onto the water. I guess all it takes is a little, and God will honor that seed of faith and meet us where we are and pull us the rest of the way. **"Peter got down out of the boat, walked on the water and came**

toward Jesus. But when he saw the wind, he was afraid and, beginning to sink, cried out, 'Lord, save me!'" Matthew 14:29-30 (NIV). How often we start sinking. Something happens to shake our faith or doubt creeps in making us question our moves. That's when we start sinking. Peter's sight in this case was actually a hindrance to his actions. He saw the wind and the waves and that's when he hesitated and began to sink. Perhaps it would have been better if it had been dark and he couldn't see those stormy waves surrounding him. If we start to sink through all the "what ifs" and hesitate or turn around…we will never get out of our boats. It takes a lot of faith (and closing our eyes to what we see and wonder about in our own minds) to just take that step of faith out of the boat. Faith is stepping out of a boat in a storm. We must keep our eyes fixed firmly on Jesus' outstretched hand and not let our attention or vision get diverted. Our only concern should be keeping Jesus in clear sight and knowing that He already knows our pathway and has it all figured out ten steps ahead of our moves. I often say that I am my own worst enemy, succumbing to doubt and fear. I must hold His hand and go forward, stepping out of the boat when called to do so. This does seem in opposition to the directive to *be still*; the answer to any contradiction is to keep my eyes focused on Jesus to know what He is directing me to do and to consult Him in prayer. **"Keep (fix) your eyes on Jesus, our leader and instructor" Hebrews 12:2 (TLB).**

(20) A Special Voice

Puppets have always been a part of my teaching and love for children. I have used puppets to "lend me a hand" in my teaching children (of all ages) and also as part of my ministry in sharing God's word over the years. Surely this has always been a part of God's unique plan for me, and one of the shades of meaning of **Jeremiah 29:11 (NLT) "For I know the plans I have for you; plans to give you a purpose and a hope."** My puppets have endearing personalities and always share jokes and humor, all qualities that share the love of God for one another and cheerful hope. These characters have been a part of me and the basis of many special relationships with others for most of my life. God will give us a voice when He wants us to speak, and it is important that we use it to serve Him. Mine just happened to be a voice of a fun-loving character that has brought much joy to my life and countless others. I am thankful for the ability to use my voice in a unique way to share God's love. *May all I ever do point to You, and may I always use my voice to speak of Your love.*

(21) To All Generations

My first grandchild has opened up a new pathway of hope for me and has grown my heart! Gabriel was born January 17, 2014, and his name means "God is my strength." Long before I knew his name or when he'd be born, that phrase was one of the messages God was using to pull me along in my health journey. Gabriel brought the fulfillment of God's word that He had some hope and a purpose in store for me. He renews my reason to write down my words to encourage others and grows my hope for health improvement so that I can be here to love on him and help to grow him in the faith. With my love for children, I know that this role has to be part of God's Jeremiah 29:11 plan and purpose to keep me around! I call the grandparent experience "love recycled" – experiencing a second layer of loving and raising children who are an extension of ourselves. **"So we, Your people and sheep of Your pasture, will give You thanks forever; we will show forth Your praise to all generations" Psalm 79:13 (NKJV).** God has us all in His hands for the number of days He has pre-determined even before we are born. It is a blessing to get to use our life experiences and lessons in faith to pass along and be a part of our children's and grandchildren's cloud of witnesses. That should be part of our parental roles, but more importantly it is kingdom work. God's call to a task includes His strength and provision to complete it. That helps me in my daily walk and the tasks to which He has called me. As I write, my second grandchild is on the way – surely making 2014 the year of *double blessings*. God knows the number and names of all of our family's next generation. May we show forth God's praise and bring them up in the way that they should go. *Lord, thank You for your hope in all forms that sustains me each day. You are my Refuge and my Strength.*

Grandchild update: Avalyn Grace was born July 27, 2014. Her name means "beautiful breath of life" and she certainly is all that and more! My heart grew again! Praise God for this little blessing bundle and hope. **"Children are a gift from God; they are His reward" Psalm 127:3 (TLB). "Every good and perfect gift is from above" James 1:17 (NIV).**

(22) A Hopeful Outlook

Waiting for healing is exceptionally difficult during a chronic illness. Will it even come at all? Yet we are to *wait patiently* – which seems like an oxymoron, a contradictory term. **"I waited patiently for the Lord" Psalm 40:1 (NIV).** This verse means that we are to watch and wait for God's leading. While we are waiting, it is important to keep our eye on the ultimate goal of where we're going and prepare more for eternity than any steps of life or getting through it here on earth. It is important to not get so caught up in the details and miss the beauty and glory that God has for us in His creation. A renewal of strength is another reward that follows waiting, trusting, and hoping in the Lord. **"Those who hope in the Lord will renew their strength. They will soar on wings like eagles; they will run and not grow weary, they will walk and not be faint" Isaiah 40:31 (NIV).**

We can choose despair or hope (or a place somewhere on the continuum between extremes), and attitude has a lot to do with healing. But the benefits of hope are so rich that it's really the best choice! I have learned from experience that hope is not just an abstract feeling but a real thing to hang onto, like the hem of Jesus' garment. To know him deeply is to feel peace and hope. It is an assurance (an outlook, a perspective) that you know, regardless of your earthly situation, where you are going and with Whom you will spend eternity. You know that you know that you know that God is with you, and that ultimate healing comes through Him. **"Let all that I am wait quietly before God, for my hope is in Him. He alone is my rock and my salvation, my fortress where I will not be shaken" Psalm 52:5-6 (NLT).**

(23) Life Verses

I was asked the question by a friend, *"How have you developed your closeness with God?"* I am thankful to have been asked this thoughtful question and to be blessed with the opportunity to be a witness for my Lord. As I pondered my answer I realized I could give it by sharing a connection between what I refer to as my "life verses" – scriptures that the Holy Spirit has breathed on me repeatedly and at critical points in my life. Those verses are like the glue that bonds my story together. These verses have also held me together throughout my journey! I will share a brief version of my God-story here, showing how these life verses have been interwoven in the tapestry:

I have always felt close to God, under the shelter of His mighty wing. I was born into God's hands and have stayed there; but His hand has gotten bigger as my understanding of all that He is has grown. I was raised in the church, but my closeness to God has grown as I have matured, and as I have realized through my life experiences how much I need Him! I never experienced a big life-changing event to turn my life to Jesus because I have felt I have always been facing Him. But my health events have been so complicated, mixed with the loss of my parents and having to stop my teaching career, that these times have found me just clinging to Jesus' garment…sometimes by a thread, yet I have not ever let go. I have always known, from the first Bible verse I memorized – **"The Lord is my Shepherd" (Psalm 23:1).** Sometimes He is all the Hope that I have – and I've realized (as the saying goes) – all that I need. **"My grace is sufficient for you" (2 Corinthians 12:9 NKJV).** Meanwhile, He is cultivating fruits of the Spirit in me, growing my faith and teaching me. He uses what happens to me to help and comfort others and display His glory. As my health circumstances have become more complex and forced me to slow down, I have had to give up my work and learn to rest in order to survive. (And resting, as it turns out, is actually hard work!) At first in this "rest season" I felt the despair of loss and stripped of everything but God. Illness brought loss of my career and many relationships, as well as my sense of purpose… not to mention the physical pain and anxiety about so many unanswered health questions. Yet, I felt God repeatedly telling me while I waited **"Be still, and know that I am God" (Psalm 46:10 NKJV).** Although waiting through uncertainty is hard to do and being still seems impossible to do at times, I turned to fervent study of God's word and an intent focus on Him. My deep reliance on the Lord gave me hope – which I realized was not in earthly answers to save me but only in God's saving grace. Hope has become my tool for waiting, knowing that God is at work within me to cause **"all things to work together for good" (Romans 8:28 ESV).** He is always at work within us and for us, weaving the tapestry together. I wouldn't have chosen my path to take this turn, but I need to trust and obey that God did. Regardless of my plans, God always has a better one – **"For I know the plans I have for you…plans to prosper you and not to harm you, plans to give you hope and a future" Jeremiah 29:11 (NIV).** In the valleys and on the mountaintops, we are to praise Him and thank Him. *This is my story, this is my song; praising my Savior all the day long!*

(24) Through it All

I would never want to walk alone and am so thankful that God walks with me and gets me through it all. Through the fire, the rain, the mountain, the valley…I know that I never walk alone. That doesn't mean that it won't be scary or painful, that I won't feel alone or in despair at times, but that I can call on the name of Jesus at any time and be lifted up. There are numerous examples in the Bible of God getting people through things. Through the Red Sea on to dry ground, through the wilderness, through the fire, and through the valley of the shadow of death… to name just a few. Whatever we go through, God will go through it with us. **"When you pass through the waters, I will be with you; and through the rivers, they shall not overwhelm you. When you walk through the fire, you shall not be burned, and the flame shall not consume you" Isaiah 43:2 (ESV).**

I often use Paul as a Biblical role model of one of God's children who suffered but did not let it defeat him or break his spirit. He went through so many trials, and his deliverance was slow and quiet. There were no great chariots of rescue or lightning bolts of escape, but God helped him through it all. Paul held onto Jesus, like I often say that I'm clinging to the hem of His garment. God's promises do not lift us from the trials, but it is *through* these very things that our faith is grown. God interweaves threads of His love into our common, everyday experiences and our trials. No matter our circumstances, we can depend on Him every time. **"He is my strength and song in the heat of the battle" Psalm 118:14 (TLB).** God is with us all through the journey, one step at a time.

(25) The Lone Tree; Rooted in Him

A lone tree standing in a field is an old tradition by farmers to leave one tree standing for shelter and shade – a place for farmers and animals to find rest from the hot summer sun. When we wonder why perhaps we've been spared and left standing like one lone tree, we need to raise our hands to Heaven in praise and spread our arms as shade for others who are weary in the battle. The Lord spares us to enable us to be a tree of rest and encouragement to others, an anchor of hope. **"We have this hope as an anchor for the soul, firm and secure. It enters the inner sanctuary behind the curtain" Hebrews 6:19 (NIV).** He comforts us so that we in turn can comfort others… **"that we may be able to comfort those who are in any trouble with the comfort with which we ourselves are comforted by God" 2 Corinthians 1:4 (NKJV).** By reaching out to others we model for them that Jesus is our true Shelter. It reminds us that we really aren't alone and that we can support one another in the journey. Plus, a firmly rooted tree is like someone in whom we can trust – whose foundation is firmly rooted in Jesus. Our roots should be in the Lord, so that we can lead others to Him. Be **"rooted and built up in Him, strengthened in the faith" Colossians 2:7 (NIV).** *Lord, help me to wait patiently (and stand like this tree with my arms outstretched as shade for others) as You work things out and together for my good. I'm always amazed afterward how I look back and realize You were knitting all things together. I know that You are the strong vine, the true tree of strength, and I am but a branch. But others might be hanging onto me because I am rooted in You. Thank You for all You have brought me through thus far and that You use me to encourage others. Help You flow through me to others.*

(26) Unhook the Safety Chain

What is the purpose of a safety chain? It is a chain on a door that acts as a double safety feature in addition to the lock. A door can be unlocked, with the chain left intact, so that the door can be opened a little way from the inside yet there is still that measure of safety barring the door from opening fully. No one can get inside until the safety chain is unhooked. Sometimes we keep a safety chain on our hearts and when Jesus knocks we peek to see who it is without letting him come fully inside. God might be trying to make a change and take charge of our hearts. He wants us to unhook the safety chain and open fully to Him. What a different image that creates to fling the door open wide and let God into your heart and be open to His plan (even if you can't see where it's going). That is total trust and obedient discipleship – especially at times when you feel tempted to put the safety chain back on the hook and guard your heart. God has our battle, as promised in **Deuteronomy 1:29 (NIV) – "The Lord will fight for you; you need only to be still."** He also understands our humanness and will keep knocking at the door of our hearts until we open fully to Him.

(27) Let Go and Let God

One of my favorite lessons that I recall from a sermon that I heard many years ago was about a teen who had the words "Let God" above his bedroom door. As I remember the story, one time in a rebellious rage he slammed the door shut and the "d" fell off the end of the phrase. He took that as a message from God to not only let God be in control of his own life but to let go of his own desires. I visually recall my pastor holding one arm up while he relayed this story, showing how we think we are giving something up to God…but until we raise both arms to hand it all up to Him, we are still trying to hang onto that control. This story stuck with me all these years. It is such a stark reminder that while we might think we are letting God have control, we have to raise our hands up and *let go and let God*. It reminds me of the verse about committing something to the Lord and once we have given it over to Him, then we need to leave it there with trust that He will do it. In fact, if we take it back and try to manipulate things, we are showing distrust in the Lord that He will handle it. This is another one of those "easier said than done" situations, but God honors obedience to His commandments. **"Commit everything you do to the Lord. Trust Him, and He will help you" Psalm 37:5 (NLT).** The promise in that verse is that *He works*. It doesn't mean it's always in the way that we ask, but that He will work on our behalf for what is best for us if we commit it to Him. Our belief and expectant trust that He works for us is what enables it to be done. He works *as* we commit…as we let go and let God.

(28) In His Quiver

"In the shadow of His hand He hid me; He made me into a polished arrow and concealed me in His quiver" Isaiah 49:2 (NIV). When we feel like we're in a dark shadow yet know we're in God's presence, it might be the shadow of God's hand as He leads us to lessons that can only be learned where He leads. Even if it feels dark or lonely, God is always there. He is keeping us nearby until His right moment when He sends us on a mission for Him that will bring Him the glory. That is when we are hidden in His quiver. The quiver is close to His side and within easy reach of His hand. We are safe. We can't see beyond that moment, but we know that we are in His hand. The shadows of darkness can be pieces of greatest growth, where we meet God and know Him to greater depths. Faith is always made stronger in the presence of the Savior. When the time is right, He will give us enough light for the next step of our journey and illuminate our path. He will draw us out of His quiver to use our situation to help others. *Lord, keep me close by Your side and hide me in the shadow of Your mighty hand. When the time is right, draw me out of the darkness and use me to bring light to others from the experience of my journey.*

(29) Be Lifted Up

As a teacher, I'm always anxious to learn new things and share with others. I read about aeordynamics and that flying into the wind increases altitude. The wings of an airplane gain more lift by flying *against* the wind, a fact that was learned by observing birds fly *with* the wind.

A bird naturally flies with the wind to gain more lift, but when it senses danger it will turn into the wind to gain altitude. Sometimes it feels like we're flying against the current, but it is in these times that God lifts us up the most. His grace is greatest when the winds are strongest. When we are lifted up to higher altitudes, it is like being lifted up above our circumstances, and our faith is made stronger. **"My flesh and heart may fail, but God is the strength of my heart and my portion forever" Psalm 73:26 (NIV).** *Lord, may I be lifted up by You in my weakness.*

(30) Hinds' Feet

"The Lord God is my strength, and He will make my feet like hinds' feet, and He will make me walk upon my high places" Habakkuk 3:19 (AMP). I had never really thought about the purpose of "hind feet" or the back feet, particularly of a four-legged creature, or that they are vastly different from the front feet! So I took a look at my dog and watched how he uses them. He braces himself against his hind feet and even though they are longer and skinnier and seem more frail than his front feet, that is where the strength lies when he needs to lift himself up or brace himself to launch into a fast move or run. My cat does the same thing when he is preparing to leap, using the strength of his hind feet to steady and then launch himself to a higher place. I picture a deer or similar animal that might climb a mountain. God equips it with strong hind feet. On a mountain those hind feet would become even more critical in his step, and they must be sturdy for the ledges and rough terrain. We need to use our "hinds' feet" to make the ascent up our mountains – and that strength comes from the Lord. He is our source of hinds' feet strength and the best resource we could hope for, to brace us for the climb. I like to picture God behind me, pushing me onward and keeping me going. The truth is, He is actually ahead of us, always in the lead.

I had not thought about the number of times that I referred to deer within this book, and as always I was amazed when God revealed something to me that He was doing for me to fuel my writing and work for Him. My husband and I enjoy taking walks together and enjoying nature. This summer of 2014 as I was putting finishing touches on this book project, we started seeing one or more deer on several of our walks. In fact, early in the summer a little one had wandered into our yard, played with our dog, and even came right up to me and let me pet it. It touched my heart so much, and then we started seeing them nightly and it became a ritual to look for and count as many as we could on our country walks. This gave me joy and peace and felt like encouraging "Godwinks." I was surprised and a bit intrigued when I even spotted a couple on a walk in the city the week I stayed at my daughter's house. They felt peaceful to me to see, and as I was telling my son-in-law, he suggested that perhaps God was using the deer as a prophetic symbol to me. Well, God has spoken audibly to me more than once during this journey, and I believe He was now giving me some visual signs of encouragement. If we can thirst for that kind of joy on earth, what more awaits us in Heaven! **"As the deer pants for streams of water, so my soul thirsts for God" Psalm 42:1-2 (NIV).** Therefore, I decided to use the deer symbol in my book for chapter numbering, signifying God's presence with us through our journeys. *Lord, thank you for signs of nature that point me to You!*

(31) God's Itinerary

Sometimes we can't see until we look back that God has led us all the way, even though at times it didn't feel like anyone was steering! He won't stop now, as He has an itinerary for each one of us with **"plans to prosper you and not to harm you" (Jeremiah 29:11 NIV).** We spend a lot of time making our own plans, but surely that makes God laugh! Our plans are never our own. It keeps us organized to make plans, but we have to remember that God has charted out our course long before we were even born! He already knows the end of the story! That's why it often seems to us that things aren't going as planned, whereas they're just not going according to *our* plans. Even if God leads us down a path at one point and then we wonder why it's taking such a drastic turn and doesn't make sense…it does to God. He is never surprised. We still try to figure it out and steer things our way, but that's when we are most challenged to trust in God's plan. It's hard to remember that He sees the bigger picture. That doesn't mean that the choices and decisions we make every day are irrelevant, but that we need to remember to consult God in our every move – asking Him in prayer what He wants us to do and then to rely on His discernment to move or act. Or to do nothing at all, which is sometimes the answer. I find that sitting back, taking my hands off, and waiting to see what God will do (or not do) is the hardest part. I give it all to Him (or so I say) and then want a sneak preview of what's to come. Yet I know He has brought me safe thus far. **"God has been my shepherd all my life to this day" Genesis 48:15 (NIV).** Maybe we can't look back and see how much God was involved all along until we are older and have more of a past to look back on, or maybe it takes a life-changing event with total reliance on God to realize it. We have to trust in God's itinerary that comes with an assurance that He will guide our steps. Our task is to follow Him in love and obedience and remember that **"We can make our plans, but the Lord determines our steps" Proverbs 16:9 (NLT).**

(32) Wrestling Prayers

"This is the day the Lord has made; we will rejoice and be glad in it" Psalm 118:24 (NKJV). Each day is a new opportunity, a new gift to be unwrapped. While it is hard to rejoice when the day starts with pain and struggle, it helps to pray for and focus on someone else. In a way that feels like I'm abandoning my prayers for my healing, but I do not look at it that way. It helps to keep my focus positive by uplifting someone else instead of feeling the weight of my own burdens.

It's not giving up, just giving it up to the One who will handle it for us. When we wrestle with something (or someone) the battle is won when the one with the most force takes over. I want the most powerful One to be God, not the enemy that tries to step in with the power of despair and discouragement. Victory in Jesus comes with faith and trust, and we actually win the victory in prayer when we stop struggling and fighting on our own – which is the focus of "wrestling prayers." A prayer in which we wrestle and fight it out by demanding our own way actually hinders the work of God and His answers. Instead, a prayer of praise and thanks to God for being with us and helping us to endure gives fuel to God to work. I have been on my knees in agony many times, and God understands and wants to hear from us at all times – so it is okay to be honest with Him because He can take it! He's bigger than our circumstances, and in fact, He already knows what's on our hearts. He wants to hear from us and honors our honesty. But at all times it is right to give thanks and praise to God *through it all*. It is just more uplifting of our own spirits and attitudes to spend time in prayer also focusing on others and getting our minds off our own situations. What good does it do to wrestle with God's plan? **"Not my will, but yours be done" (Luke 22:42 ESV)**, Lord. What He asks of us is to bring our needs to Him; then remain still until He does His work, doing nothing that He has not commanded us to do. While it is difficult to not wrestle with our problems and leave them alone, trust in God assures us that we are in good hands. None of us knows what a day will bring, but we can approach it as a gift to be opened and praise the Lord *through it all*.

(33) I Come to the Ocean Garden

I feel particularly close to God at the ocean – a place where I feel I can cultivate His presence. It is one of my favorite spots on earth, what I would consider a "heavenly" view and sound. (I wouldn't mind if Heaven looked and sounded like the ocean!) I always have some good prayer, praise and conversation time with God while at the ocean. The tide always reminds me of God's relentless love abiding with us. Just as I can depend on the tide to still be rolling in and out each time I return to the ocean's edge, so does God's love always remain. The ocean has a peaceful magnetic quality that draws me into reflection. It is like my garden at home, a setting where I find peace. Why did Jesus go to the Garden of Gethsemane? Was it His haven? A place of peace where He felt closest to God, to pour out his heart to Him? He pleaded there with God that if it be possible to take this cup from him**…"My father! If it is possible, let this cup of suffering be taken away from me." (Matthew 26:39 NLT)**. In my "ocean garden" haven I feel more open to have that kind of honest conversation with God. I like to look out across the ocean as far as I can see, to what looks like the edge. As I look at the horizon of the ocean I feel like I am at the edge. How far does it go? I've been out there and know that the ocean is vast. But life looks that way from the outset, too, or when things are going okay. We just keep going and make plans without thinking much about the "far edge." But it has been a difficult journey lately with pounding waves. Just like the ocean, the waves seem to keep rolling in and crashing on the shore of life. How long can this go on? How long should I just take this? Do I have a choice? *If it be possible, Lord, could You take this cup of suffering from me? Yet, Your will be done, not mine.* The ocean brings forth some begging along with that deep reflection as I bare my soul before God. I must feel so at home there that I feel comfortable enough to ask that question. My ocean garden brings forth the deepest reflection from within me where I best cultivate God's presence, and He discloses His word to me. I love to let the waves wash over my feet and remember that God's love always abides, just like the firm foundation of the shore remains under my feet although I sometimes feel the sand slipping away. I know that God holds onto me firmly through life as the tide ebbs and flows and sometimes it feels like the sand is washing away beneath my feet. But I know that I stand on the solid Rock, my Lord, and not the shifting sand. We all need a place like this to come to and commune with God one-on-one. It is good to be able to come to the garden alone, just as Jesus did. *Thank You, Lord, that I can feel close to You at the ocean, in the garden, wherever You call me to walk closely beside You.*

"Your love, Lord, reaches to the heavens, Your faithfulness to the skies. Your righteousness is like the highest mountains, Your justice like the great deep" Psalm 36:5-6 (NIV).

An ocean devotional written at the ocean (a favorite family spot – Myrtle Beach):

God's power calms and soothes us, and it also encourages us when we consider its might. The ocean is a visual and sensual reminder of God's love and power. I can never imagine that someone could look at the beauty of nature like the ocean, a mountain, a sunset…and not see the handiwork of God. **"When I look at your heavens, the work of your fingers, the moon and the stars, which you have set in place, what is man that you are mindful of him; and the son of man that you care for him? Yet you have made him a little lower than the heavenly beings and crowned him with glory and honor" Psalm 8:3-5 (ESV).** I am so grateful for this beauty, yet I am not deserving to even look upon it! It humbles me and makes me feel small…and thus my problems seem small. I give God the glory for the solace that the ocean always brings to me along with the sweet memories and feelings of closeness to my parents. I have many happy memories of time spent vacationing in Myrtle Beach with them, and now how my family enjoys time here together. As I look out at my familiar view of the ocean I am once again in awe of the power of the water and God's love. Just like God's constant love, the ocean remains the same with the relentless spilling of waves onto the shore. No matter how long we are away (and even visiting other ocean spots…) the waves continue to roll. It can also be "moody" as the weather changes and the waves crash onto the shore with fury. Sometimes it deposits new treasures on shore to find and enjoy. Those can be good or not-so-good surprises! Life does all that. Yet God's love is as constant as the motion of the ocean, giving us an anchor to hold onto through life's waves, storms, treasures and surprises. **"Give thanks to the Lord, for He is good; His steadfast love endures forever" Psalm 136:1 (ESV).**

(34) Harmony

Harmony occurs when everything blends together to produce a pleasing result. It is sweet, peaceful and desirable. We long for harmony in our relationships and in the details of our lives. But we appreciate harmony even more after we have experienced disharmony. How would we know that the major chords are so sweet unless we have heard minor keys? Being a pianist, I remember the arduous scale exercises of my childhood years of piano lessons. The major scales were easier and much more pleasing to the ear! But the minor keys offered a more solemn, somber mood and have their place in creating music just as much as the happier, melodic major keys. The same goes for the black and white keys on the piano. A black key produces a good sound on its own, but when you play a white key next to it the sound is a little more pleasing. If you press a white key and a neighboring black key at the same time, they produce a very disturbing sound – a "discord." Likewise, the notes of a chord create a harmony because they work together to create a pleasing sound. A major key has a more pleasing and harmonious sound than a minor key. But you can't fully appreciate the major/minor key harmonies unless you can hear the difference. If I play the black keys on my piano, the notes can be just as beautiful as the white ones (as long as I hit the right ones at the right time and in harmonious combinations). Yet to fully demonstrate all that the instrument can do, I must press them all. So it is, that in our lives we have to experience discord to appreciate the harmony. We must endure all kinds of experiences (major and minor) but will count it all as blessings from the Lord to know that He is the giver of all circumstances and is with us through it all. God doesn't waste a hurt or a pain but wants to use it. I use my health experiences to be a witness and a vessel of encouragement to others. I cannot keep silent from praising God (and playing the piano) to tell of all that He has brought me through and how He sustains me. True, we tend to lean on God more heavily when we are in pain or darkness or difficulty. But a finely tuned heart for God will lean on Him all the time, praising Him *through it all, no matter what.* **"Sing and make music from your heart to the Lord, always giving thanks to God the Father for everything" Ephesians 5:19-20 (NIV).**

(35) Drink Your Cup

I often wonder how I got here – on this mountainside. After all the years of education and training and experience…to have to "retire" early due to health complications. *Surely this isn't what You had in mind for me, Lord?* Um…correction; surely it isn't what I had in mind for me! There I go again thinking this life is about me and my plans! But honestly, had I known that I'd be stopped in my tracks with this disease business just five years after completing my doctorate degree, surely I would not have felt compelled to climb that mountain. At that time God had opened a door, closed another, and it was under His direction that I took the path that I did. While it was a tough climb, dare I say that this health one is even harder! To be still, do nothing, and wait… that is a bigger challenge than all my studies! I know that I am stronger and richer in relationship sense – and I'd never give up the friends that I made with colleagues and students I have trained to be teachers (and many still friends) and the lives I touched through teaching. Not to mention the work ethic that I modeled for my children. They are all high achievers, and particularly my eldest daughter, Tiffany, has taken on the teaching role. I am proud to think that she followed in my footsteps, and I believe I even influenced my husband to enter teaching as a second career in life. I just would not have chosen to be stopped in my tracks and to lay down my teaching tools, when I had hoped to have more years of teaching ahead. I might never understand until I get to Heaven, and then just when I can ask "WHY?" I imagine I'll be so in awe of the majesty of being before God and being able to praise Him in His presence and to be reunited with my loved ones…that I'll surely forget the question and it won't matter anymore! *Lord, I keep climbing this mountain because I know You are there!!!*

This is when I remember that my plans are not my own and that if this is God's will, who am I to question it? Shall I not drink this cup and be thankful? **"Shall I not drink the cup the Father has given me?" John 18:11 (NIV)**. Drinking the cup means doing the will of God. If He instructs us to climb a mountain, we should climb it; take a different path, take it. Sometimes it's not a huge assignment or as monumental a task as a mountain, but just dealing with the hand that we are dealt. That is how I have learned to deal with a chronic illness – do the best you can and take one step at a time (with God). Even when we suffer while drinking this cup, we are doing God's will to trust and obey His direction. He will never, never, never, never, never leave us. (The Greek translation of **Hebrews 13:5** actually lists it with five "nevers" – that is extra, extra measures of assurance!) We will see the result of God's handiwork. There are no medals, trophies, or degrees for the highest form of attainment, which is the reward that comes from doing God's will. So we drink the cup we are given and trust that it is all according to God's plan! I am often reminded by others that I *am* still teaching, just in a different form – through my writing, sharing and encouragement. Besides, we never know how far that influence reaches. My favorite teaching quote speaks to that: "A teacher affects eternity; he can never tell where his influence stops" (– Henry Adams).

(36) Dead Ends

I think it is natural to wonder why bad things happen to good people. But dare I ask if we are *good* people? Or, perhaps the actual question is: Aren't we all *good* in God's eyes? He does love all of us unconditionally, after all! The perplexing circumstances are ones in which there seem to be no way out; no resolution. A chronic illness (for example), feels like a dead end. Or maybe worse than that, like running through a rat maze with just the same ole, same ole thing at every turn. It feels like you'll never reach the exit. How long will this last? Good ole Paul (whom I refer to so often) had several experiences where there seemed to be no way out. This caused him to reason that bad things happen **"that we might not rely on ourselves but on God" (2 Corinthians 1:9 NIV).** Bad things are not a new phenomenon. When God led the people of Israel out of Egypt, He deliberately took them by way of the Red Sea. It wasn't an easy path but the way God wanted them to go – even back then and for all of time…God had a plan! They couldn't see it, but they had to trust Him to guide them. When they got to the edge of the Red Sea, it surely appeared to be a dead end stopping point. Besides that, the Egyptians were hot on their trail, catching up to them! The only direction they could look was up, and when they did so, God parted the waters and led them to safety through the sea. I'm pretty sure that when the waters divided, opening up a pathway, they scurried across, not looking back! When there appears to be no escape route, the only direction to look is up. How often I wish I would look that direction *before* I get to the dead end point, but I guess it's those times that cause us to rely even more heavily on God. It's then that we realize how much we need Him. *Lord, help me to rely on You in all the times – good and bad – and not just when I've reached a dead end. I know that You are always there, the One and Only way out! Help me to stay on the path You have chosen for me. Thank you even for this mountain climb that brings me closer and closer to You.*

(37) Let God Steer the Boat

I struggle in my storm, at times feeling like I'm rowing alone. That is when I realize that I'm trying to steer! I need to remember that God is in my boat just as He was with the disciples on that stormy night as it tossed them about in the wind and the waves. Those are the kinds of times that we are fearful and feel alone in the storm. Jesus had told them to get into the boat and cross over to the other shore. They thought they were the captain of their own ship and would choose their own course. When the wind picked up they still tried to manage on their own. Fear overtook them. They were pouring all their strength into rowing the boat in the storm and getting nowhere in the process. Meanwhile, Jesus was waiting on the shore, ready to hear His name and jump in the boat with them. He wasn't going to jump in and force himself into their situation. He never left them out of His sight, as He waited patiently and watched them. He knew just the right time to come to their rescue. Late at night, Jesus took a couple steps onto the water and as if they had never seen Him before, the disciples were scared! They were astounded and afraid at the sight of Jesus walking across the lake to meet them! Had they forgotten who He was, and what He could do? (O, ye of little faith!) **"Immediately He spoke to them and said, 'Take courage! It**

is I. Don't be afraid.' Then he climbed into the boat with them, and the wind died down" Mark 6:50-51 (NIV).

How many times are we of weak faith like that? How often do we keep trying to row our boat in the storm on our own, forgetting what God can do? We put all our energy into trying to make it to shore instead of looking up to see that Jesus is right there. We wait until we're being tossed about in the storm to reach out and rely on God, trusting that He will save us. God is walking on water all the time around us. In the perfect moments of our pain, God will speak to us. He feels the depth of our storm and is the only One who can calm the waves. He jumps into the boat, and the storm dies down or at least is manageable. He will always give us the strength to endure. I guess we're human to try to steer our own boats and life is going to be full of storms. Jesus is in the boat with me despite how bad the storm might seem. I cannot steer this crazy life boat on my own! *Lord, I've been battered by a storm for a very long time now. Help me remember to let You steer my boat! Help me to look up and realize You are there, My Courage, with strength and an outstretched hand.*

(38) A Good Recipe – Jesus is the Center

Anyone who knows me well knows how much I love to bake, and luckily my family enjoys reaping the benefits! This is a family trait passed down from my mother and her mom, and I often use their recipes (particularly for pies and cookies). At this point, I know some of those recipes by heart. Unfortunately there is no recipe in life to guarantee us freedom from pain and suffering; but like some of those recipes that I know by heart, memorized scriptures can work like recipes for the heart. Scriptures sustain me at the hardest times and are like good recipes to help my heart to call on Jesus. I am thankful for the firm foundation of Jesus.

"So then, just as you received Christ Jesus as Lord, continue to live your lives in Him, rooted and built up in Him, strengthened in the faith as you were taught, and overflowing with thankfulness" Colossians 2:6-7 (NIV).

God wants us to keep our eyes and focus on Him – the true Center. God's word, firmly rooted like a good recipe committed to memory, is the best remedy for the toughest times. After all, how do we know when the center of a baked good is done? When the center is firm!

(39) Make Me a Blessing (or a Lark!)

"The Lord God is my strength and my song" Isaiah 12:2 (NLT). I haven't given up, but while I await healing I also wait upon the Lord to use me – to make me a blessing to someone else each day, or at the very least as often as possible! Focusing on troubles makes us too self-centered, but with a focus on God first and foremost, He sends us to walk alongside others. Sometimes I'm overwhelmed with where God leads me and what He gets me into (like the saying, "Be careful what you ask for!"), but I just know that He is using me. I want my life and my words to always point to God, and may everything I do praise His name…for anything I do is not of my own strength or power anyway! I have heard that a blessing is a prayer for a future blessing, so what an offering it is to be able to ask for that on someone else's behalf. A simple outreach that I like to do is to honor others on their birthdays by sending a card and reminding them that they were created on that day in God's image and for a reason. Birthdays are the perfect time to ask for a future blessing for someone. The sweet part of that is only God knows in advance what that will be! On my own birthday my daughter (Kelsey) sent me a thoughtful message, and I asked her if I could share her encouraging words: *I prayed for any specific words for you and your life, and the Lord gave me the word "Lark." I thought maybe I just misheard, but I decided to Google the lark and see what came up. Whoa! What an encouraging prophetic word from the Lord over your life! I found that larks are well-known for their beautiful songs, and are one of the only birds to sing while in flight, not just while sitting or resting. Therefore, they often signify cheerfulness and the ability to find joy in the midst of "flight" or in the midst of everyday life. This is something I think you are great at, and that you continue to grow in – just finding the simple joys of life regardless of what you are doing, and being able to sing even when you're in the midst of everyday life, pain or monotony. Larks also symbolize being the bringer of warmth, light, and life – something you do for others who need it on a daily basis! You're a great encourager and friend, and you take time to love the least of these. Larks also typically symbolize hope! The Lord is going to bring you such hope this year, and He is pleased with your desire to lift up others with hope and encouragement. May He develop these lark traits in you in ways you don't even foresee for this year!* I share that humbly, and while I do not feel deserving of her abundant words, if the Lord chooses to use me as an instrument of blessing like the lark symbolizes, then I want to make the most of it! May the Lord continue to be my Strength and my Song (like the song a lark would sing) for all of my days. **"Let your light so shine before men, that they may see your good works and glorify your Father" Matthew 5:16 (NKJV).**

(40) Waiting / Tapestry Weaving

Times of illness require waiting on the Lord. **"I waited patiently for the Lord; He turned to me and heard my cry" Psalm 40:1 (NIV).** I'd love to say that I wait patiently, but I feel that is a contradiction of terms. But waiting is the secret of strength and hope. I look to God to provide the resources for me to wait patiently, for He is my true Strength. Only *in Christ alone* can I wait. This Psalm means to watch and wait for God's leading, which translates to not doing anything that hasn't passed by God first. **"Blessed is the one who waits" Daniel 12:12 (NIV).** But waiting for healing and waiting for God to work out His plan is always hard. I consulted scripture for the steps to godly waiting, which includes threefold instruction: *Wait in prayer. Wait in faith. Wait in quiet patience.* This tells me that I have to *pray it through* on my health journey, hush my spirit to wait and let God work, all the while knowing that He is never late and has the full tapestry in His view, weaving it together in His time and fashion.

Throughout this waiting period, I have been reading about how God weaves a tapestry through the events of our lives. I see glimpses of how God is doing this in my life. Perhaps with age comes the ability to look back and see how God has always had a plan and was piecing my life together. Perhaps it is from my view and vantage point on the side of the mountain that I can better see the tapestry coming together. I have had to work hard on my trust and faith that *God is working all things together for my good* (from **Romans 8:28**). I know it and say it…but we all surely can admit that in the toughest times it's hard to believe it really is all *for good*. That's when we have to say "Your will be done, Lord" and "in Your timing," and *I trust that You will never leave me or forsake me* (**from Hebrews 13:5**). Those are all promises proclaimed in scripture for us to lean on and remember. They come to me over and over as tools for my trust toolbox to keep me equipped for the journey. Other words that keep washing over me are **strength** and steadfast **perseverance** – more tools that are needed to keep climbing and to remind me that it is all worth it to meet Jesus. **"Be steadfast, immovable, always abounding in the work of the Lord, knowing that your labor is not in vain in the Lord" 1 Corinthians 15:58 (NKJV).**

There is a German proverb that says "Begin to weave and God will give you the thread." In my case, I believe God dangled the thread in front of me and said basically, "Do something with this." He was telling me that while I was waiting I was to use my struggle and experience for good – which should always be to help someone else. I feel this is the essence of God's command in **Luke 6:31 (NIV)** to **"Do to others as you would have them do to you."** In fact, He more specifically told me to write a book! So I took that thread and started weaving this work together. As it has taken shape, so have I – through digging deep into God's word and getting closer to Him all the while. Meanwhile, I try to wait with confident faith and patience, keeping my eyes fixed on God – who is my full joy and the Tapestry Weaver of my life. *Lord, make me what I should be in the midst of my afflictions; help me to live within them, for however long they last, always upheld by Your hand.* **"Amen. Even so, come, Lord Jesus!" (Revelation 22:20 NKJV).** For this, we wait with hope.

Never Travel Alone

Never travel the road alone
Even if you think you know the way.
Let the Lord always be your guide,
For by your side He'll stay.

You might have to choose your pathway;
One way has several lanes, the other has few.
Choose the one the Lord would take,
Let Him guide you what to do.

Your path may take a sudden turn;
You didn't think it'd go that way.
But the Lord knows your destination
And what's in store for every day.

What's beyond the next mountain?
Will it be a smooth or bumpy ride?
You'll find it doesn't really matter
If you have the Lord at your side.